ENCOUNTERING

Heaven

and the

Afterlife

ENCOUNTERING

Heaven

and the

Afterlife

—— ✳ ——

James L. Garlow *and* Keith Wall

BETHANY HOUSE PUBLISHERS

Minneapolis, Minnesota

Published by Bethany House Publishers
11400 Hampshire Avenue South
Bloomington, Minnesota 55438

Bethany House Publishers is a division of
Baker Publishing Group, Grand Rapids, Michigan.

Printed in the United States of America

In keeping with biblical principles of creation stewardship, Baker Publishing Group advocates the responsible use of our natural resources. As a member of the Green Press Initiative, our company uses recycled paper when possible. The text paper of this book is comprised of 30% post-consumer waste.

green press
INITIATIVE

Library of Congress Cataloging-in-Publication Data

Garlow, James L.
    Encountering heaven and the afterlife : true stories from people who have glimpsed the world beyond / James L. Garlow and Keith Wall.
       p. cm.
    Summary: "True stories of spiritual encounters and near-death experiences offer glimpses into what happens when people die, written from a Christian perspective"— Provided by publisher.
    Includes bibliographical references (p.   ).
    ISBN 978-0-7642-0811-9 (pbk. : alk. paper) 1. Near-death experiences—Religious aspects—Christianity. 2. Future life—Christianity. 3. Spirits. I. Wall, Keith A. II. Title.
    BT833.G37   2010
    236'.2—dc22

2010011014

— ✳ —

To Christopher Garlow (1988-2009),
whose life continues in heaven and whose legacy
continues on earth.

–Jim

To Juliana and Logan–
May you know that this life is just a small part
of a very big adventure.

–Keith

Contents

Part Seven: AN EYE TOWARD ETERNITY

Visions and divine signs provide a peek into the afterlife.

Your Personal Invitation to . . .

Adventures in the
Afterlife

Let's take a hypothetical excursion: Suppose you and your spouse completed the paperwork for a new life insurance policy—but health care being what it is these days, the company requires more than just a stack of signed forms and an at-home blood draw from a visiting nurse. So this morning you are scheduled for a physical at your doctor's office.

Once there, you find yourself being poked and prodded by your physician. She presses a stethoscope to your chest, wraps a blood-pressure cuff around your bicep, and asks about your family history and other potentially embarrassing questions. So far, so good. But this kind of physical requires something more: You've got to complete a brisk walk on a treadmill, with electrodes taped to your chest and attached to a nearby monitor.

Okay, you can do this. You consider yourself to be in reasonably good shape. What's a little uphill climb on a moving conveyor belt?

But twenty minutes into the test, with the treadmill's speed increasing as quickly as your drops of perspiration, something seems wrong. You feel pressure in your chest. Tightness. Like someone has put a bigger version of the blood-pressure cuff around your upper torso and started to inflate it. Then you notice a tingling sensation in your left arm. Suddenly lightheaded and nauseous, you stumble off the treadmill and collapse on the cold tile floor.

Fade to black.

The next thing you know, you are in a different place. It's not your doctor's office, but it still feels *medical*—stark walls, antiseptic odor, chrome-plated instruments, fluorescent lights, and lots of scurrying, unfamiliar people wearing white and green. They're also wearing concerned expressions. Furrowed brows, narrowed eyes, clenched teeth.

It's you they are concerned about. You realize you've been taken to an emergency room. A tall woman with graying hair utters the words *myocardial infarction*. Huh? Someone else says, "heart attack." Oh, that.

You notice that you're lying on a gurney, metal guardrails at your sides, a spider web of tubes and wires tangled around your limp body. Strangers frantically turn knobs, push buttons, jab needles into your flesh. Then you hear it . . .

You've heard the sound in movies and lots of those hospital dramas on TV. It's the EKG machine that suddenly spews out a shrill, high-pitched blaring noise, reminiscent of your smoke detector at home. You look over just in time to see the once-jumping, squiggly line go flat.

Fade to black once more.

Now the questions begin. Assuming the above scenario really happened to you (and it's certainly a possibility for any one of us), what do you think comes next? The physicians and other medical personnel swarming around you, despite their best efforts, declare you dead. Now what? You're going to have the adventure of your life, that's for sure.

Yes, some people are lucky enough to get resuscitated. But what if you weren't among the fortunate who "died" and lived to tell the tale?

Researcher Dinesh D'Souza asks the question that has been on the minds of human beings for millennia:

> Is death the end, or is there something more? This is the ultimate question. It has been the defining issue for entire cultures from the ancient Egyptians to the present. And in truth, there is no more important question that any of us will face. It is the issue that makes every other issue trivial. If you have doubts about its significance, go to a hospital or a funeral or talk to a parent who has recently lost a child. You will discover very quickly that the apparent normalcy of everyday life is a sham.[1]

What happens the moment you die? Where will you end up? How will you get there? When you arrive, will you know people? Will angels escort you to your next destination? What are heaven and hell really like?

The scene described above is not far off from a real-life drama that unfolded in the life of Earl Foster, pastor of Faith Community Church in Shady Hills, Florida. For him, the prospect of flatlining on a gurney was anything but hypothetical. On March 16, 2006, Earl, age sixty-three, lay on a table at New Port Richey Hospital while medical personnel began a blood transfusion. Suffering from diabetes and a condition that causes low blood counts, Earl had accepted this procedure as a necessary requirement to keep him well.

But something went wrong. Terribly wrong.

A few minutes into the procedure, his heart stopped, and in an instant he found himself up in a corner of the room watching as physicians tried to shock him back to life with a defibrillator. From his hovering position, Earl felt a vague sense of disappointment at their attempt to revive him, and he wasn't sure why exactly.

A split-second later, he discovered himself no longer in the hospital room, but somewhere indescribably beautiful. An overwhelming sense of peace swept over him. He knelt beside a stream to drink the cool, clear water from his cupped hands. Across a lush meadow, he saw his old dog, Ram, running as fast as he ever did and leaping over the meandering brook to greet his owner. Earl's long-lost cat, Puff, came scurrying up behind. As Earl reached out to meet them, he spotted his sister, Margie, with both legs perfectly okay and working fine—even though she had died with only one leg.

Following her down the grassy hill were his mother and father, happy and healthy, with no signs of the heart attacks that had ended their lives on earth. Soon Earl was surrounded by his grandparents, looking much younger than he'd ever seen them, and a welcoming horde of aunts, uncles, cousins, and friends. Everyone appeared so robust and full of unmistakable joy.

"Right then I realized that complete healing lies ahead for every child of God," Earl said. "The blind will see exquisite vistas, the deaf will hear blissful music, cancer will disappear, and the illnesses and ailments of old age will vanish."

It suddenly occurred to him why he felt disappointed that the medical personnel were trying to jump-start his heart. He didn't want to return to his earthly life. Now he knew he never wanted to leave this place. But soon enough, he woke up to find himself back on the hospital table. Thanks to the miracles of modern medical technology, Earl had no other choice but to conclude: Heaven can wait.

Earl's near-death experience (NDE) and glimpse of paradise echo thousands of similar stories. His vivid recollections—as clear in his mind as yesterday's golf game or trip to the coffee shop—give us all a foretaste of things to come.

For most people, one NDE would be astounding. A life-changing event, to be sure. For Earl, though, a repeat performance lay ahead, only with a different encounter on the other side.

A year and a half later, on August 26, 2007, Earl was back in the same hospital for another "routine" blood transfusion. Apparently for Earl such commonplace procedures are anything but routine. Once again his heart stopped and, as he was later told, he had no measurable signs of life for two minutes. This time, he immediately felt surrounded by light and propelled forward.

Suddenly he was stopped by someone who stepped in front of him. Earl recognized his brother, Robert, who had died the previous year of cancer. He put up his hand and said to Earl, "It's not your time. You have to go back. You have to endure. You must continue on with your life."

Disappointed, Earl asked, "Why do I have to continue on? You didn't."

"You still have work to do, and I squandered much of my time," Robert said. "You still have work to finish. You have to keep on."

Then Earl asked him, "How will I know when I am finished? Will it be soon?"

Robert said simply, "You will know!"

Earl desperately wanted to ask what it was he had left to finish, but he abruptly regained consciousness on the treatment table. A physician stood over him, paddles in hand, while nurses bustled about. He had—once again—been shocked back to life.

In the pages ahead, we'll present to you more than thirty stories like Earl's, and not only about near-death experiences leading to a glimpse of heaven (or hell). We'll also tell of deathbed scenes where the final visions of dying people open a window, ever so briefly, into the next world. We'll share the experiences of men and women certain they were visited by deceased loved ones. We'll highlight the unexpected visions and spiritual insights that offer unique perspectives on the afterlife. We'll show that angels and demons travel from the spiritual world to our physical world, either to help or harass human beings. We'll even share tales of ghost appearances.

This isn't a book filled with comprehensive explanations, convincing elucidations, or cogent expositions from the Bible. Rather it is an eclectic collection, offering an intriguing look into the lives of ordinary people who have had extraordinary spiritual encounters. But you'll find much more than poignant and gripping tales: You'll gain a peek into the (usually) invisible world that surrounds us every second of every day. Gathering insights from a wide-ranging compilation like this is akin to working a jigsaw puzzle. Most people complete the flat-edged border and then go about fitting together piece after painstaking piece—until at last the picture is whole. When you read a single story in this book, you'll hold a puzzle piece in your hand, a small but vivid portion of a much larger picture. By the time you've read all the stories, you'll have a fairly well-rounded understanding of the afterlife.

We'll be right up front with you: Some of the topics covered here will bolster your beliefs and fortify your faith—but others will challenge and stretch your thinking. Who knows—some may make you angry. We acknowledge that some of the issues presented are controversial and may elicit incredulity. The Bible, our ultimate source of spiritual wisdom, is clear and explicit on many areas, but vague or silent on others. It is up to each of us individually, with God's help, to seek the truth. Our hope is to open a helpful dialogue, not a heated debate. More so, we hope to open minds and hearts to the reality that the spiritual world is real, buzzing and swirling all around us. (The last book we wrote together, *Heaven and the Afterlife*, covers a wide range of topics and is jam-packed with explanations, theories, and theological perspectives to help guide you through confusing or controversial issues. It would be a useful companion to the book in your hands.)

In addition to stimulating discussion and thought, our purposes for presenting these fascinating narratives are to demonstrate that:

The division or distance between the physical world and the spiritual world is incredibly thin—like tissue paper. It's probably more accurate to say there really is no distance. Beings with bodies and beings without occupy the same space, just on different planes. Sometimes there's sufficient overlap—or a door thrust open between worlds—to offer the opportunity for physical and spiritual entities to meet face-to-face. Further, there's much more two-way traffic between this world and the next than most people realize. The accounts in Part One of this book provide anecdotal evidence that people regularly do make a round trip from earth to heaven (or hell) and back again. According to the Bible, and supported by eyewitness testimony, angels and demons frequently leave their domains and interact with humans.

The more we learn about life beyond the here and now, the less likely we are to be unnecessarily fearful. We know the majority of people fear death—and many are downright terrified of it. When we understand that dying really is a matter of "crossing over" to another place, we're empowered to face our own death, or even the death of a loved one, with courage and peace. The spiritual encounters of reliable individuals supply us with valuable insights into what lies ahead. For those who have placed their trust in God, an amazing new place awaits us. Scripture assures us that "God is love" and "love casts out fear."[2]

The mystery and magnificence of God make life (this one and the one to come) an amazing adventure. There will always be skeptics among us, those who come up with rational, scientific explanations for spiritual phenomena. But those who have spiritual faith—those who acknowledge there's much more than what we can see, taste, smell, hear, and feel—should remain open to the possibilities that God works in our world in surprising and unexpected ways. Why should we limit the vast, creative, and unpredictable God who created heaven and earth and everything in between? Solomon wrote, "As you do not know the path of the wind, or how the body is formed in a mother's womb, so you cannot understand the work of God, the Maker of all things."[3] Through stories we gain hints, glean clues, gather inferences that help form our beliefs about the afterlife. But there will always be mystery and intrigue about the supernatural world—at least so long as we reside on *terra firma*. This is a book that embraces the unknowable mysteries of God and his creation, even as we explore what is knowable through the real experiences of reliable people.

Most of all, we hope these stories point readers to the living and loving God who desires a close relationship with every person on earth. As the apostle John wrote in his New Testament gospel account: "For God so loved the world that he gave his one and only Son, that whoever believes in him shall not perish but have eternal life. For God did not send his Son into the world to condemn the world, but to save the world through him."[4] That is the very essence of any discussion or dialogue we have about the afterlife—God has prepared an indescribably wonderful place for you to spend eternity, and he wants to enjoy it with you.

Doubter . . . or Questioner?

Jim Garlow

I have a confession to make: I am an unlikely candidate to write this book. I have never had a near-death experience. I have never had a glimpse of heaven. I have never, thankfully, had an up close look at hell.

Further, I have never seen an angel (as far as I'm aware of). I have only once seen a *fully* demonized man. Only one time have I been attacked by a demon, or at least that is what I think occurred.

Unlike the people in the pages that follow, I have never had an unusual "visitation" of any kind. Although I have been a pastor for decades, I have no personal deathbed scenes about which I can write. I have never seen a ghost. The one opportunity I had to witness one, I promptly and cowardly passed up.[1]

And what about dreams and visions? Only three, frankly. I have had thousands of dreams—all of them jumbled, generally wacky, and largely forgotten by the time both feet hit the floor. But I have had only three experiences that would qualify as *bona fide* dreams or visions in so many years of ministry, all of them long ago.

Thus, I am an unlikely candidate to publish a book on these topics. And the experience of my coauthor, Keith Wall, is not totally unlike my own. He has had several "strange coincidences" that point to dramatic spiritual involvement in his life—but, like me, nothing that has been in-your-face obvious and apparent.

There is another reason I am an unlikely candidate to coauthor this book. My greatest struggle in my Christian faith is not the "normal" temptations I have observed in others. Instead, for as long as I can remember, I have privately battled an internal and persistent question, "What if all I believe is wrong?"

I don't consider myself an intellectual, but my Christian struggles have been primarily in the intellectual arena, as opposed to the "temptations of the flesh" that seem to plague others. In fact, truth be known, the likely reason I continued on an academic journey that included three master's degrees and a doctorate of philosophy in historical theology was because of the nagging thought, *What if all I believe is wrong?* I wanted to make sure I knew truth.

Flowing out of that question emerged a favorite biblical personality: Thomas. While preachers railed on Thomas for being the "doubter," I identified with him. He was my hero! And still is.

As you might recall, Thomas was not present when Jesus first appeared to his close circle of friends. When they announced to Thomas that Jesus had in fact been resurrected, Thomas responded with an understandable, "Unless I see [for myself] . . . I will not believe it."[2] Others call that doubt. I call it smart! I would have said the same thing. Thomas was not a doubter. He was a questioner. And as such, he wanted the facts.

In contrast to the wonderful Scripture passages to which many tend to gravitate, the one that remains among my favorites is: "I do believe; help me overcome my unbelief!"[3] I have lived with the tension of those two seemingly conflicting claims from age nine to the present.

In the end, the evidence for Christ and the Bible was and is so breathtakingly convincing: The Bible is true. God is God. Jesus was born of a virgin, lived a sinless life, was crucified, died, was buried, and rose on the third day, and is coming back to rule this world. And, yes, there is a heaven and a hell, and everyone is going to one place or the other.

There is another reason that I am not a likely candidate to write a book on the ethereal realm. I am an amateur historian. My last two academic diplomas were in the area of history, which is something quite tangible. History pertains to events that have occurred within time and space. But some of the accounts you are about to read seem to defy both, at least at times. I feel quite comfortable with time and space. "Heaven and the afterlife" sometimes seem—how do I say this?—intimidating, daunting, and nebulous topics.

It is important to distinguish between being rational and *rationalism*. Being rational is a good thing, as the mind is one of the greatest of God's creations. *Rationalism*, in contrast, is arrogance in assuming that *only* what I can know (see, taste, measure, quantify, and so on) and understand is real.

In summary, I approached this project with a healthy dose of well-founded skepticism. Along the way, Keith and I used reasonable and consistent vetting techniques. To accept stories as valid, one of us either needed to know the people personally—with firsthand knowledge of their integrity and credibility—or we had to know someone with a high degree of reliability who could vouch for the person being profiled. In those rare cases where we did not have such knowledge (which was only one or two instances), contact was made with a credible pastor or person in leadership to discern the character of the storyteller. Furthermore, the other criterion was that the individual had to be still living. We did not want to rely on secondhand information, even from people we knew to be trustworthy.

We admit we are not social scientists—we are, in a real sense, reporters. In contrast to our previous book, *Heaven and the Afterlife,* in which we presented in-depth explanations and scriptural discourses, we offer few theological or practical assertions regarding what you are about to read. We are following the proverbial "we report, you decide" approach.

In fact, we concede that we do not know how to explain many of these accounts. And we feel no compulsion to do so. Our response to some of the stories, perhaps like yours, is "Could this really have happened? How is that possible?" But we felt it was not our place to tamper with the stories, to somehow fit them into our constructs or preconceptions.

We do have deep convictions and make no attempt to hide them. We believe the Bible to be absolutely true, in everything it says and affirms. We believe the Bible is a reliable guide for every aspect of life, particularly as it pertains to the pathway to heaven. We believe the Bible is the Word of God. In fact, you will see that we affirm scriptural warnings—in both our books on this topic—when we make the case that a person should never attempt to communicate with the dead, as that is clearly and strictly forbidden in Scripture.

Keith and I approached our first book on heaven, hell, and related topics with great inquisitiveness, not fully certain of all the pathways we might take therein. We approached our second book with a low-grade skepticism, a sort of maybe-but-maybe-not mental framework, uncertain of what we might encounter.

The process involved a division of labor. I threw out the net to gather stories, followed up with hundreds of contacts, prodded for details and nudged for information, and vetted individuals we wanted to profile. I then classified and codified the nearly four hundred accounts that came in. Using a team of wonderful assistants, we developed a system of categorizing and rating for completeness. It was at this point that my enthusiasm for the project really grew. What we were uncovering was a gold mine. With hundreds of credible accounts emerging, we began to see consistent patterns. People, unrelated by time and geography, were reporting remarkably similar experiences.

I cannot tell you the number of times someone said or wrote to me, "I have never told anyone this, but . . . " Or "I know people might think I am crazy, so I have told very few people."

Once the stories were collected, Keith began the challenging task of selecting which ones to include. Then he began the process of interviewing and writing that resulted in the book you now hold in your hand.

Remarkably, only three featured individuals chose to use pseudonyms. One did so to protect another person in the story. Two others preferred to remain anonymous because they know that the rationalism and skepticism of their colleagues would jeopardize their professional calling. It is sad—but probably not surprising—that their co-workers might believe that nothing could possibly exist that they cannot scientifically measure.

I have close personal connections to many of the individuals featured in these pages. But the account to which I am most personally tied is a story we debated including—the death of my nephew Christopher Garlow in a fiery and truly freak car catastrophe (see the story "Never Far Away"). This occurred only one day after the official release of *Heaven and the Afterlife* and a short time before I began work on its follow-up, *Encountering Heaven and the Afterlife*. The devastating experience brought all of these issues into vivid—and tragic—clarity for me.

As you will learn, I had sent advance copies of *Heaven and the Afterlife* to my brother and his family. After Christopher's passing, I learned that he and his family had read our book and discussed heaven at some length.

As I write this new book on the afterlife, emotions are still raw for me as an uncle who performed the funeral. But they are especially so for my brother's still-traumatized family. It is for that reason that I dedicate this book to Christopher Garlow who, on July 16, 2009, at age twenty-one, encountered heaven and the afterlife.

PART ONE

Eyewitness Accounts

People who have had near-death experiences bring back
vivid descriptions of the pathway to paradise
and descent into darkness.

If you were to travel back in time a hundred years and ask your great, great grandmother what she knew about NDEs (near-death experiences), she'd probably give you a blank stare. Question her about flat-lined EKG readouts, "clinical" death, and heroic emergency-room resuscitations—and she would think you'd been nipping at the mulberry wine again.

But if you were to ask her to tell you the stories she's heard about people who'd had a brush with death—the ones who saw beautiful bright lights, visited with long-dead relatives, or felt a sense of overwhelming peace and love, Granny would most likely smile and say, "Oh, *that*! Why didn't you say so?"

Although modern medical technology has made it possible for *more* people to "die" and return with tales of incredible out-of-body journeys, the truth is, it's been happening throughout human history. Literature records variations on the experience from nearly every culture on every continent. It is only in our time of mass communication that such accounts have entered the mainstream of our collective conversation about death and dying.

That trend picked up speed in 1975, the year Dr. Raymond Moody put his professional reputation as a psychiatrist on the line and published a little book called *Life After Life*. In its pages, he attempted to tackle a question that most serious scientists wouldn't touch with a ten-foot pole—though it has haunted human beings for millennia:

What happens when we die?

After studying the firsthand accounts of hundreds of people who had "crossed over" and returned—that is, people who had survived a life-threatening crisis, sometimes after a complete loss of measurable vital signs—Moody coined the phrase *near-death experience* to describe the phenomenon. Most intriguing was the fact that the stories he gathered were remarkably similar to each other. He found that while no two NDEs are identical, most had one or more core elements in common: a feeling of being out of one's body, moving through a tunnel toward a bright light, and encounters with angelic figures or deceased loved ones.

Other far less frequently reported stories reveal decidedly dark and hellish experiences. Dr. Maurice Rawlings, author of *To Hell and Back*, believes such traumatic NDEs are vastly underrepresented in literature, giving the impression that death is always a doorway into bliss. In his view, the mind quickly walls off painful memories, so that hellish experiences fade from conscious awareness much faster than positive ones. Furthermore, he says, "Hell cases also remain unreported because of personal ego and the embarrassment of it all. Patients don't want to discuss a matter that confirms ultimate failure in life, an overwhelming defeat, a slap in the face."[1]

Early research by Rawlings, Moody, and a few other pioneers in the field triggered a veritable avalanche of interest in examining such stories for clues as to what lies on the other side of death. Since then, dozens of studies have documented thousands of NDEs among people from various religious traditions, demographic groups, and cultural backgrounds. Scientifically minded researchers have looked for purely chemical or biological explanations for the extraordinary experiences survivors describe. They've analyzed oxygen deficiency, blood pressure, drug-induced hallucinations, and even the final, frantic firings of synapses in the brain—just to name a few possible culprits—in search of a mechanistic cause for the NDE.

That thinking dominates the medical profession as well. Doctors are trained from day one to purge their practice of anything that isn't scientifically verifiable—an unfortunate attitude that has done more than anything else to suppress open-minded NDE research.

In his book *Evidence of the Afterlife: The Science of Near-Death Experiences*, Dr. Jeffrey Long, an oncologist and NDE researcher, writes:

> I heard far too many stories of the problems NDErs encountered when they tried to tell their near-death experiences to the medical staff. One of the classic stories was a patient who told his doctor about his NDE in front of several nurses. When the patient finished telling his story, the doctor looked up from his clipboard and said, "Don't think too much about it. It was just fantasy."
>
> When the doctor left the room, the nurses closed in around the crushed patient and said, "It's not fantasy. We hear about these events all the time from patients. Doctors like him live in fantasy. They never hear these because they don't listen to their patients."[2]

Still, in spite of so much highly motivated reductionist research, science has failed to identify a smoking gun to disprove what NDE stories strongly suggest: that human consciousness—what theologians call the soul or sometimes refer to as the spirit—survives beyond bodily death. In fact, as you will see in the following pages, people who have been there often report a heightened and enhanced quality to existence that is far beyond mere "survival." Most speak of feeling *more alive* while out of their bodies than they ever have before. They experience tremendous freedom, unconditional love, and indescribable peace on the other side. They commonly want, more than anything, to remain there—and they only come back out of a sense of compassion for their families, unfinished business on earth, or simply because they are given no choice by loving beings who turn them back with the words, "It's not your time yet. You have more to do."

If nothing else, NDE survivors have convincingly challenged the popular nihilistic notion that *nothing* awaits us when we die but a permanent "lights out." Not true, they say. Every single person who has crossed over and returned—and thousands of these accounts are available—would say emphatically that there is absolutely, definitely, unquestionably a world beyond this one.

We collected the stories that follow to offer glimpses into the afterlife. Like single drops of rain that become part of a mighty river, each story contributes something vital to our understanding.

Jesus said, "In my Father's house are many rooms; if it were not so, I would have told you. I am going there to prepare a place for you."[3] NDE stories may not give us a detailed floor plan of the place he has prepared for us, but they at least offer a tantalizing peek through the window. They teach us important things about how to live in *this* life, how to grieve the loss of someone we love, and what to expect when the moment of our own death arrives—as it will for each of us, without fail.

I

Heaven on Wheels

—— ✳ ——

A Harley-Davidson motorcycle, a tragic
accident, and a trip to the afterlife that changed
Abby Cleghorn's life forever.

Six feet tall, with a salt-and-pepper goatee and boyish smile, Win
treated Abby like a queen. He told her he loved her with all his heart,
and indeed she'd never felt as loved in her entire life. Win gave her
strength, helping her move past the painful memories of the abusive
marriage she'd once been in. They got engaged in November and
made plans to marry after the New Year.

One Saturday morning in December, they took Win's truck over
to the Applebee's restaurant in their hometown of Aiken, South Carolina, meeting up with friends for the annual Make-A-Wish Foundation
Christmas party. Win and Abby brought toys and visited with the
kids. It was a wonderful morning.

That evening, it was back on the motorcycle and a short ride into Augusta for the Harley-Davidson Christmas party. As Win steered his bike up the highway, Abby wrapped her arms tightly around his waist and smiled.

Unexpectedly, Abby saw her mother first, and then her sister. She wasn't on the motorcycle anymore, but standing beside two women. Abby shouldn't have recognized her sister at all, since Patty Lynn had been stillborn two years before Abby was born. But there she was, a woman who looked to be in her thirties; and Abby, forty-four, knew immediately who she was.

Abby's mother was the first to speak. "Abigail," she said, "It's not your time. You need to go back to be with your kids and your grandbabies."

Abby said, "Yes, ma'am." But she didn't move. Go back? How in the world was she supposed to do that?

Her sister said gently, "Abigail, did you hear what Mama said?"

"I did," Abby replied, "but I can only go so fast."

Patty Lynn urged, "You need to quit talking and get going."

Abby turned and saw a field of the greenest grass she'd ever seen. Walking toward her, arms outstretched, was Win.

"C'mon, baby," he said in the playful drawl that had always melted her heart. "We're going to be late."

"But I can't go with you, Win," she responded. "Mama told me to go back."

"I don't think you want to go back, Abby," he said. "You don't know how hard it's gonna be for you. If you go back, you're going to have to be very strong."

"I can do it," she insisted. "I'll have the Lord with me, helping me along the way."

Win paused and said, "If you do go back, I want you to do something for me."

"What is it, Win?"

"I want you to remember that I love you with all my heart."

The next thing Abby remembered was lying in a hospital bed, hooked up to monitors and beepers. Sitting in a chair next to the bed was Tabi, one of Abby's stepdaughters from her previous marriage.

Tabi seemed overjoyed. "Mama, I'm so glad you're awake! I wanted so badly to tell you the news."

Abby blinked. "News?"

"While you were asleep," Tabi enthused, "I found out that I'm pregnant!"

"Abigail, it's not your time," Abby's mother had told her. *"You need to go back to be with your kids and your grandbabies."*

Abby, still groggy, struggled to form the words. "You found out last night? Who finds out they're pregnant in the middle of the night?"

"I didn't find out in the middle of the night. Mama, you've been asleep for five weeks."

What Abby didn't know was that on the evening of the Christmas party, she and Win had been just three blocks from home when a car driven by a teenager veered into their lane and hit Win and Abby head-on. Win died at the scene of the accident. Abby was thrown fifty feet and had to be airlifted to a hospital. In the helicopter, she died three different times and was resuscitated. She suffered severe injuries to her brain and throughout her body. She'd spent the next five weeks in a coma, surrounded by friends and family.

Two visitors practically lived at the hospital while Abby was in her coma—a woman and a young girl Abby had never met before.

The pair was the mother and sister of the young man whose car had killed Win, and they visited Abby's family almost daily.

Shortly after Abby awoke from her coma and learned that Win had died, one of the nurses said, "Abby, someone is here to see you. The boy who was driving the car that hit you is here with his family. What should I tell him?"

Most of Abby's memories of life before the accident were gone. She could barely remember the man she had promised to marry. In fact, her clearest memory of Win was standing with him in heaven as he'd said, *"I want you to remember that I love you with all my heart."* She was trying to remember that he loved her, but it was a tall order when she could barely remember their life together at all.

Her brain injury had also affected her emotions. Abby couldn't seem to muster any feelings, including sadness or even loss. She didn't remember how to cry. Even so, the thought of meeting the young man who had been driving the car that had taken so much from her evoked a strong wave of . . . something. Anger? Regret? Resolve? Unable to put a name to it, Abby looked at the nurse, who was still waiting for her answer.

"Tell him no," Abby said. "I can't see him. Not today. Maybe not ever."

Abby spent the next two months living with her daughter Beth, who was devoted in taking care of her mother, and five more months living with Tabi. Abby was in a wheelchair, and her left hand had been paralyzed. She had lost all depth perception. The greatest injury had been dealt to her brain. In addition to losing all her emotions as well as memories, she couldn't remember to do simple things like take her medicine or eat.

Even recollections of things Abby had done or known most of her life were gone. One day she and her stepmother, Pearline, were driving home from one of Abby's frequent doctor appointments when

Pearline suggested grabbing something to eat from McDonalds. Car idling, they sat at the drive-through window. Abby was silent.

"Sweetheart," Pearline said, "you need to tell me what you want so I can order for you."

Abby looked blankly at her stepmom. "But I have no idea what kind of food they serve here."

Recovery was slow as Abby relearned how to walk. Because of the brain injury, she had to focus on one thing at a time. Even breathing took conscious effort, and sometimes Abby forgot. Family and close friends knew to remind her, especially if she called them on the phone in a silent panic.

Her most meaningful victories came as she began to reclaim some of her memories and eventually some of her emotions as well. One day Abby opened up the file on her computer containing all her photos. Looking at pictures she'd taken of Win and the many places they had visited, she felt a few of her own memories starting to stir. Her emotions, however, took longer to heal.

For two years Abby felt nothing. Looking back, she says now that it was as if she didn't know how to have a feeling. On the two-year anniversary of the accident, she sat in her living room, looking at the wall where she'd hung a photo of Win. Suddenly she felt a lump in her throat. The next thing she knew, she was crying. It was a major breakthrough. After several minutes, though, Abby realized something was wrong. She could feel it in her chest. Tears still forming small rivulets on her cheeks, she picked up the phone in a panic and called one of her girlfriends. As soon as the woman saw Abby's name on caller-ID and heard the silence on the other end of the phone line, she knew what to do. "Breathe, Abby!" she said firmly. "Breathe!"

Some days Abby thought about her last conversation with Win. He had told her, *"I don't think you want to go back, Abby. You don't know how hard it's gonna be for you."* As she struggled to reclaim her life, there were days she wished she had listened to Win and stayed right where she was.

One Sunday morning, Abby was watching the television program *Hour of Power*. On that show, a woman shared how she had been driving on the freeway when someone on a bridge threw a bottle of acid at her car. It not only broke her windshield, but the acid also splashed all over her, leaving her disfigured. She talked about how, in time and with God's help, she had found freedom from bitterness, even finding it in her heart to forgive the assailant.

Abby often attended church and prayed, but she'd never been one to feel any consistent direction from God. At that moment, though, it was as if God gave her a nudge. She went to her phone. With a few calls, she obtained the number of the family of the boy whose car had changed the trajectory of her life forever. Speaking to his parents, Abby said, "I'd like him to know that I forgive him. Can you give him that message for me?"

One evening soon after that, Abby was in a restaurant. As the waiter refilled her water glass, he commented on how the best part of his job was getting to meet interesting people who had done unusual things.

Abby laughed. "You haven't heard anything yet! I died after a head-on collision and have been to heaven!"

The young man stared. "Tell me more."

Abby told him her story. As she finished, tears filled his eyes. "My brother died six months ago," he said. "I've been so worried about him, but you've given me comfort and hope. I can't tell you how much that means to me."

Abby left the restaurant convinced that she had just experienced a divine appointment.

On another occasion Abby was at her doctor's office, when she found herself in a conversation with a technician. After hearing about Abby's visit to heaven, the woman said, "I know you were meant to be here today and to tell me your story. My dad died about eight months ago, and my mom has been so upset she hasn't even been able to go into their bedroom. I needed to hear your story so I could tell it to her."

Before long, Abby noticed that almost everywhere she went—doctors' offices, restaurants, coffee shops, hardware stores—she met people who had questions about death or about God. Time and time again, they found comfort in Abby's story of what she had experienced.

One day Abby told a friend, "Before the accident, I was close to the Lord, but I can't say I took the time to really listen to anything he was saying to me. Now I hear him on a regular basis, telling me to share my story with the folks he brings across my path."

Today Abby walks with a limp. She still has limited memories of her life before the accident and continues to have to relearn the most unexpected things. "I wasn't feeling well recently and went to my doctor. He said, 'Are you feeling nauseated?' I told him, 'I have no idea what that word means or what it's supposed to feel like.'" She laughed. "It wasn't until I threw up in his office that we figured out that, yep, I'd been feeling nauseated!"

Win is buried in Williston, twenty miles from where Abby lives today. She has never visited his grave and says she probably never will. "I don't need to see dirt," she explains. "I can see dirt anywhere. I know where Win is. I've seen him there."

Abby continues, "What Win told me in heaven came true. Coming back was harder than I ever thought it would be, and I needed to be strong. Without my experience in heaven, I don't think I would have been strong enough for what was ahead of me, what lies ahead of me still. But what I told him in heaven was true too: *I can do it. I'll have the Lord with me, helping me along the way.*"

After she saw Win in heaven, Abby got a tiger-paw design tattooed on her ankle. Win graduated from Clemson University, and the paw print is the logo of their mascot, the Clemson tiger.

It's a symbol of strength, to be sure. It's also a reminder of the man who once gave her the courage to love and whose parting words gave her the courage to live. Abby says it's in honor of someone waiting for her on a field of the greenest grass she's ever seen—someone who loved her with all of his heart and, she believes, loves her still.

2

"An Angel Picked Me Up and We Flew"

————— ✳ —————

Four-year-old Kennedy Buettner was dead
at the bottom of a swimming pool for nearly
fifteen minutes. Or was he?

On June 15, 2000, the Buettner family—Craig and Amy and their five small children—had just one thing on their minds: *baseball*.

Little League baseball, to be exact. The oldest of the kids, ten-year-old Jacob, was a member of the top-seeded team in that year's championship series. Craig, a Tuscaloosa family physician and the University of Alabama football team doctor, was serving as assistant coach. As they prepared for the first game that afternoon, expectations were high. The adults decided to give the boys extra incentive by promising to throw a swim party that evening—*if* they won.

They lost.

When Craig and Brad, the head coach, saw how disappointed

everyone was after the game, they quickly decided to have the party anyway.

"When we told them that, the boys were so happy," Craig said. "Turns out they were more upset about not getting the swim party than about losing the game."

Forty people, most of them children, crowded into the backyard of one of the team families that evening. The father, George, grilled hot dogs and hamburgers while the rest of the parents supervised the kids in the pool. When it was time for dinner, everyone was herded out of the water and into the yard, where they sat on towels and blankets.

Craig settled his kids down with plates of food. Four-year-old Kennedy, in his baggy red swimsuit, sat on a nearby towel with other children. Amy focused her attention on their five-week-old baby, Mark. Craig brought Amy a hamburger and finally sat down himself to enjoy a few moments' relaxation before the party moved back to the pool.

"I took one bite and felt like God gently tapped me on the shoulder and told me to find Kennedy," Amy recalled. "Somehow I knew before I ever turned around and looked that he was not on that towel with his brother anymore."

She was not terribly alarmed at first. As the mother of five small kids, she had learned long ago not to panic every time one of them wandered out of her sight. Still, Amy felt an unusually strong sense of purpose as she got up from her place and began searching for her son.

Her first stop was the pool. Kennedy had taken swim lessons and was at ease in the water. He might have somehow slipped back inside the fence while no one was looking. She searched all around the pool. No Kennedy. She walked to the front yard, calling his name as she went.

Still, no luck. Amy returned to the backyard and told Craig about the situation. He joined the search. Like Amy, he searched around the pool first for a glimpse of a little red swimsuit. Seeing nothing, he went inside to where Kennedy might have gone to play with toys. Outside again, he got distracted when one of the other children was run into by a tricycle and needed his attention.

Then Craig experienced the kind of horrific moment that haunts a parent's nightmares. He heard Jacob screaming, and ran to find him:

"Daddy, Daddy, we found Kennedy! He was at the bottom of the pool!"

Fear seized Craig. As a doctor, he was well prepared to deal with emergency situations. But he also knew the horrible implications of Jacob's words. He expected to have to jump in the water to bring Kennedy to the surface. When he arrived, he was surprised to see his son lying on the concrete at the pool's edge. Jacob and two other young boys had already dived in and retrieved him from beneath nine feet of water in the deep end. Kennedy was out of the pool—but the sight of him added to Craig's growing alarm.

His son had been underwater for more than twelve minutes.

The boy's body was deep blue. His skin was bloated and his belly looked like he was "nine months pregnant." He wasn't breathing and had no pain response. His pupils were dilated and unresponsive.

"Those are all the things I look for when I pronounce somebody dead at the hospital," Craig said. "Why I didn't want to just sit there and hold my child in my arms and cry right then, I don't know. Somehow the Holy Spirit gave me the power to ignore what my eyes saw and believe that my son wasn't really gone."

While others around him got on their knees and started praying or quoting passages from the Bible, Craig immediately began to administer CPR. After two and a half minutes, Kennedy still had not responded. At five minutes, he began taking erratic breaths on his own. Between five and ten minutes, the boy began to thrash around and exhibit behavior that doctors call "abnormal posturing," a kind of muscle seizure that indicates severe brain damage—and usually precedes death.

At eleven minutes, paramedics arrived.

———————

Amy Buettner knew Kennedy was gone the moment she saw him. His leg felt like "cold rubber" to her touch.

But that didn't stop her from praying for a miracle.

"I fell on my knees and cried out to God, *'Please don't take him; I'll have him any way you'll give him to me.'* I didn't stop praying for an instant."

After a few minutes her hope revived, as she saw Kennedy start to breathe and move. But when she observed him posturing, she knew what it meant. She had seen that before.

Six months earlier, Amy had been at the bedside of her brother, Mark, when he died of brain cancer. For many months, she had watched him slowly succumb to the disease, which left him horribly scarred and incapacitated. Just before he died, at age thirty-five, Mark was seized by posturing spasms that she later learned resulted from a loss of brain function when someone is near death.

Mark had been the Buettner kids' favorite uncle. A Louisiana native, he was an avid deer hunter and outdoorsman. The kids called him "Uncle Buckmaster." His loss had been a severe blow to the whole family.

Still Amy prayed, "Lord, I know you are the true physician. I know you can heal my son."

Several hours later, Craig and Amy arrived at the intensive care unit of Children's Hospital in Birmingham, Alabama. While Kennedy had been transported from Tuscaloosa in a Lifesaver helicopter, they traveled the fifty miles by car—a trip that seemed to take, Craig said, "about five years."

Kennedy was now on a ventilator and attached to an array of IVs and instruments. He was restrained and paralyzed with special drugs to keep him from thrashing around in the bed and injuring himself further.

The doctor in charge did not sugarcoat the assessment he gave the Buettners that night. Based on clinical measurements of Kennedy's condition, he estimated the boy had only a 15 percent chance of survival. If he lived, there was only a 1 percent chance he'd recover to lead a normal life. In the bed next to Kennedy lay a girl who'd also drowned. She was still in a coma after three weeks.

"At that time the guilt and fear absolutely overtook my body," Amy said. "Why didn't I see him go to the pool? I felt like such a horrible mother. I accused myself of not giving him enough attention as the middle child, of not reading to him as much as I did the older kids when they were young, all those kinds of things. It felt like Satan had his claws sunk into my shoulder."

For her, the next forty-eight hours were a blur: meetings with doctors; nursing the baby, Mark; and fighting desperately to hang on to hope. On the third day, Amy was alone in the room with Kennedy, her Bible open on the bed. She asked God what she should read, and the answer came to her: "Today is the eighteenth of June—read Psalm 18."

As she read, one verse leapt from the page as if it were lit up in neon: "He reached down from on high and took hold of me; he drew me out of deep waters. . . . He brought me out into a spacious place; he rescued me because he delighted in me."[1]

"It was like a switch turned on," she said, "and I just knew that God was going to draw Kennedy out of 'deep waters' and rescue him."

That day doctors discontinued Kennedy's pain medication and removed his restraints.

Craig's faith "switch" was flipped the next day. He had noticed that ten-year-old Jacob was withdrawing deeper and deeper into himself as time went on. The boy blamed himself for what happened to

Kennedy. "What kind of a big brother am I not to protect him?" he asked his father in despair. "It's my fault."

Craig escorted him to Kennedy's bedside. In spite of his critical condition, he looked much better than he had the last time Jacob had seen him—at the side of the pool. He was conscious, but just barely.

"There we were, crying and talking about ordinary stuff. I was explaining to Jacob what all the machines were for. Then I said to Kennedy, 'Little buddy, let Jacob know you're going to be all right, will you?' And even though he was still being artificially paralyzed, his left arm lifted up, reached across his body, and gave us a thumbs up. It was like electricity passing through our bodies when we saw that little thumb go up in the air. We knew God had told us Kennedy was going to be okay."

A while later, as Craig was sharing with Amy what had happened, he looked down at the plastic hospital bracelet both he and Amy wore while Kennedy was in the ICU. What he saw stopped him mid-sentence. The name of the doctor who had been there when Kennedy first arrived, but whom the family hadn't seen since, was *Mark Buckmaster.*

"To me it was one more sign that God was in charge and that everything would be okay. From then on, he got better and better."

Later that day doctors took Kennedy off the medication keeping him immobile. He still had a ventilation tube down his throat but was responding with nods and head shakes to questions. The attending neurologist was at a loss to explain what he was seeing.

"Are you scared?" Craig asked his son.

He shook his head. *No.*

On Tuesday doctors reluctantly took him off the ventilator. He coughed and sputtered as the tube came out of his throat. His voice was hoarse, but he was in good spirits. Amy held him in her arms for the first time. She could finally ask him the question that had haunted her for five days:

"Baby, what happened?"

His answer was not what she expected to hear.

"I was in a whirlpool, then an angel picked me up and we flew," he said, in his quiet, gravelly voice. "We flew through walls, and I flew through *you*, Mommy."

On Thursday—one week after arriving at the hospital with a 99 percent chance of being paralyzed and severely impaired cognitively for the rest of his life—Kennedy Buettner went home. That afternoon he played baseball, gingerly, with his brothers and sister.

Over the next few days, Kennedy talked more about things he had experienced after he went into the water.

"I was very, very careful not to put words in his mouth," Amy said. "I just let him tell me about things in his own way and in his own time."

Craig added, "As he told us where he went and what he saw, he would look to the left and right and even point, like he was remembering physical places he'd been."

The following conversation is compressed, having taken place over several days:

> *When the angel picked you up, where did you go?*
> I went to heaven.
> *What did you see?*
> I saw Jesus. I saw lots of people and angels. They were very happy.
> *Did you see Uncle Mark?*
> Yes. He looked just like Jesus. All his boo-boos were gone. He was happy. I saw a door with jewels on it. There was snow on the other side when they opened it.

"When he talked about what happened next, Kennedy got very quiet," Craig said. "He spoke in a whisper."

I saw a volcano, and there was a Pokémon[1] in it. No, it wasn't really a Pokémon, I've never seen that one. It was a dragon.

Was the dragon happy or sad?

He was happy. He looked at me and growled.

Were you scared?

No, I was with Jesus and Uncle Mark. I was standing on glass and I was invisible.

Was the volcano part of heaven?

No. (His tone seemed to imply, No, silly . . .) It's not part of heaven. There were lots of people in the volcano. They were very sad.

How did you get back?

Uncle Mark pushed me down, and an angel brought me back. You know, Mommy, Jesus is coming back here.

"I'll never forget how his little finger pointed down at the ground when he said, 'Jesus is coming back *here*,'" Amy said. "And, no, he didn't say when," she added with a smile.

Kennedy made a full recovery without ever suffering a setback. Ten years later, he has no negative residual effects from his brush with death. He is physically and academically normal–he's especially good at math. He plays on his school basketball team and enjoys tennis.

As a medical doctor, Craig admitted, "There is no science behind his recovery. I saw the X rays and the test results myself. The neurologist on his case can't explain it. This experience taught me vividly that life is so very fragile, but God is totally sovereign. In my practice I don't act like I have all the answers anymore. Now I know anything is possible."

For Amy, there is solace in knowing her brother, Mark, is healed and happy in heaven. She also takes comfort from the fact that, even in the grip of a potentially frightening death, Kennedy didn't suffer and wasn't afraid.

"There was no sting of death for him," she said. "All Kennedy remembers was he was in a whirlpool—which might have been the sensation of water swirling around him—and an angel picked him up. There was no struggle and no pain. He went straight to heaven."

The Buettners share their story every chance they get, but they stress there is nothing special about their family. Their purpose is to reveal what God did for them.

"We are the least qualified people in the world to talk in front of people," Craig said. "But it's not about us; it's about the plan God has for every one of us. It is about asking people, 'If you die today, do you know what comes next? Do you know where you will spend eternity?'"

3

To the Edge of Hell

——— ✳ ———

**When Ron DeVera "died" during open-heart
surgery, he woke up to his worst nightmare.**

Ron DeVera stepped carefully to keep his footing on the last patches
of packed snow at the edge of his driveway, the crusty remnants of a
storm that had blanketed Cleveland in early November 2008.

He was loading luggage into the back of his car and looking
forward to celebrating Thanksgiving in two days with his mother,
Helen, and stepfather, Richard, at their home in Columbus, a two-
and-a-half-hour drive away. He always welcomed the chance to be
with family—and was also glad for a break from his government job
at the Defense Finance and Accounting Service.

Ron's wife, Julia, buckled their two children into the back seat of
the car, a boy and a girl, five and two. Julia grew up in the former Soviet

Union where she had become a licensed physician before emigrating to the United States. Here, her education qualified her to pursue a career as a registered nurse.

The sun was shining that day, and the air was crisp—chilly, but not bitterly cold. Ron started the car, pulled onto the street, and drove away without a backward glance. He had no reason to suspect he was heading toward a date with eternity, no clue it would be weeks—not days—before he returned home. There were no signs warning him that this journey would take him *much* farther than he planned.

He was about to go to the edge of hell and back.

———

The road trip itself was uneventful. Traffic was light, and the kids weren't as restless in their seats as usual. The family arrived at their destination and spent a relaxing evening of engaging conversation over a good meal. Finally, the kids were tucked in and the adults were getting ready to call it a day as well. Julia had already retired to the guest room. Ron was on his way to join her when he felt a twinge of discomfort in his chest.

The sensation wasn't dramatic, not like a full-blown heart attack that strikes with sudden, excruciating pain. Even so, the mounting pressure Ron felt in his chest summoned his undivided attention. He stopped in his tracks in the hallway as the tightening continued to build into a dull ache. He held his breath for what seemed a long time, then exhaled in deep relief when the pain began to subside and the pressure disappeared.

He continued on to the bedroom, where he told Julia about the incident. She sat up in bed like she'd received an electric shock, suddenly wide awake. As a medical professional, she knew all too well the implications of what her husband described.

"She didn't hesitate," Ron remembered. "She said, 'You need to get to the hospital. Right *now*.'"

Her urgency might seem like an overreaction, until one knows something about Ron's history with heart disease. Beginning in 2002, he had received medical treatment for significant blockages in his arteries almost like clockwork, every two years. He'd undergone multiple angioplasty surgeries, in which doctors inserted a balloon-like device into the clogged artery and inflated it to stretch the tissue. They'd left stents behind to hold open the passages. To make matters worse, heart disease was common among the men in Ron's family. His father died of a heart attack at age forty-two, along with two of his brothers—Ron's uncles—at forty-two and forty-three.

"It was simple chemistry with me," Ron said. "By this time I was eating healthier than ever, less of the bad meat and more vegetables and fruits. But there was no denying I was high risk."

His first thought when the pressure struck: *Not again!*

Still, by the time he told Julia what had happened, he felt much better. The pain and pressure were gone. He promised to go to the hospital in the morning if the discomfort returned. She reluctantly relented.

But at breakfast, the pain *did* return.

Richard drove Ron to the emergency room at a nearby hospital. Once aware of Ron's history, the ER physicians wasted no time admitting him for tests and observation. They quickly came to a troubling conclusion: Angioplasty was no longer an option. Ron had blockages of at least 70 and 80 percent in two arteries—in one instance in spite of a stent put there to prevent such a recurrence. The only remaining course of action was open-heart surgery to perform a quadruple-bypass operation.

Surgery was scheduled for the following Wednesday. Ron would spend Thanksgiving in the hospital.

Over the next several days of waiting, Ron pondered what might happen if he didn't make it through the surgery. He asked the hospital administration about executing a power of attorney and making out a will. They set him up with a staff lawyer who helped complete the necessary paperwork. He talked with Julia about whether the kids should come to visit him in the hospital. Though he wanted to see them, Ron decided against it—not wanting to be seen in his vulnerable and weakened state. He worried about insurance policies and mortgages and whether Julia and the kids would be taken care of if he died.

The one thing he never considered was what dying might mean for his soul. He never took inventory of his relationship with God.

Ron had gone to church regularly as a young man, but had stopped after disagreeing with some of the hypocritical practices he observed. After many years, he had recently found a congregation near his home and was attending services again—"once in a while." The whole issue of religion and salvation lay on the periphery of his life. So much so that, even lying in the hospital awaiting major heart surgery, Ron didn't stop to consider what might await him on the other side should something go wrong.

"It never really crossed my mind to talk to God," Ron admitted. "I figured, what was there to worry about? I didn't do evil things. I wasn't thinking about all the sins I had committed. I thought being basically a good person was enough. I was wrong."

The morning of the operation loomed cold and cloudy. The time for Ron's surgery came and went, since the patient on the table before him was in the operating room longer than expected. The minutes ticked by. Julia was there, along with Helen and Richard. Finally, Ron's turn came. Nurses put him on a narrow gurney and wheeled him through labyrinthine hallways to a set of double doors leading to the OR—a boundary his family couldn't cross. They said their good-byes and expressed love for each other. When his family had gone, the nurse briefed Ron about what to expect on the other side of the double doors. The next thing he knew, he was looking up into bright surgical lights. The process of getting prepped for surgery is a blur in his memory. He remembers voices, towels, IV needles, and then . . . darkness.

When Ron woke up, he was confused. Something wasn't right. He remembered where he was *supposed* to be—in the hospital recovery room. He looked around expecting to see familiar faces and feel a comforting touch. What he saw instead filled him with horror and stone-cold dread. He was in the middle of a dark forest. In every direction there were dead, barren trees against an ashen sky. A sticky "black gook" hung like moss from the ends of the twisted branches. He knew instinctively he would suffer great harm if the stuff ever touched his skin.

But that was not all he saw. Among the trees—reaching to the horizon all around him—lurked a virtual army of grotesque demons. Hundreds of them. Disbelief and confusion gave way to raw terror.

"Some of the demons were small, like gargoyles, with horns and claws," Ron recounted. "Others looked more like humans, except they were terribly misshapen. One close to me had something growing out of its back and sides—something like bones, but twisted and deformed."

Ron couldn't hear a single sound, but he saw the demons' lips moving and knew they were communicating with each other. Those nearest him suddenly fixed their attention on him and started moving slowly in his direction. One of the human-sort sat down beside him, and Ron immediately experienced a stabbing pain in his right hand. He couldn't see his own body, but clearly felt the demon press its claws into his flesh, torturing him just for the pleasure of witnessing the pain.

"I felt such panic," Ron said. "I thought, *This is it. I'm going to be tortured for the rest of my existence, and there is nothing I can do about it.* I knew if I didn't get out of there, they would keep me forever."

Then he had another thought: *"I don't belong here. I'm a good person."*

Unable to move or flee, Ron called out to God for help. He barely recalls the words he prayed in pure desperation, but his plea was a heartfelt cry for deliverance from his tormentors. He asked God to lift him out of there and to make the demons go away.

The moment he prayed, they began to disappear. The small horned ones were the first to go. The taller human-looking variety seemed stronger and required all his focus and attention to resist. For what seemed like hours and hours—maybe days—he prayed. He still couldn't hear any sounds, but was intensely aware of the hatred the demons felt for him. Some of them would disappear when he prayed, only to be replaced by others. He fought on, continuously pleading with God for deliverance.

"There were so many," Ron said. "After a while I got extremely tired, just fighting to stay awake. Eventually, I couldn't do it anymore, and I fell asleep."

When he awoke again, the demon-filled forest had vanished. Instead, he found himself in a small, dark cave, the walls and ceiling pressing in on him. And he was not alone. Five or six demons lay on top of him in the cramped space, their weight pressing down on his chest with suffocating intensity. These creatures were different in appearance from the others he had battled for so long. They looked human but were translucent and ghostly white in color. The most striking feature of each of the demons was a pair of hideous, bright red eyes looking at Ron. Some of them were male in form and others looked female.

"My first thought when I woke up was that I'd failed," he recalled. "I thought in terror that these would be my tormentors forever. Those horrible eyes were redder than anything I'd ever seen. They were doing disgusting things to each other. I knew if I didn't escape somehow, they would start doing them to me too."

Once more, Ron refused to give up, clinging to the thought that he didn't belong there. He began to pray again, asking God to save him from the demons. He prayed with all his might and, as before, they started to disappear. Yet even as they were fading from sight, the weight of their bodies seemed to grow heavier and heavier until Ron feared he would be crushed. He cried out to God more fiercely than ever.

Suddenly a bright light broke into the darkened cave. He heard ordinary human voices around him—the first sounds he'd heard since he awoke in hell. The demons were completely gone now, and Ron was filled with assurance, at last, that he would recover. God had answered his prayers.

Ron DeVera's surgery was supposed to take only four hours. After twelve, his exhausted doctors were finally satisfied they had accomplished what they set out to do. But as soon as they began to close him up, Ron flatlined.

"I died on the table, and they had to open me back up," Ron said. "They shocked me three times to restart my heart."

Afterward, he was unconscious for ten days. During the first five, doctors kept his chest open, ready for emergency intervention. Later, Ron learned from Julia that nurses had to tie him down at one point because he kept struggling to get out of bed. He had no difficulty imagining what could make him do that.

After he woke up, Ron had only one thing to say to the medical staff: "I want to be baptized—*now*."

"When they saw I was serious, they said I was crazy," he said. "They told me about the risk of infection and all that, but I didn't care. All I could think about was getting things straight with God."

The physicians' arguments prevailed, and baptism had to wait. But not for long. Once he was released from the hospital, Ron arranged to be baptized by sprinkling at his mother's Methodist church on the Tuesday before Christmas. The pastor insisted on meeting beforehand to be sure Ron understood what he was doing and why. It was a formality that, in Ron's case, was hardly necessary. He knew exactly what was at stake. Hell was no longer an abstract concept to him. It was a vivid and harrowing reality.

After the ceremony, Ron told his story to the group of twenty or so people in attendance. He's told it many times since then.

"You can see in their eyes that most people don't really believe it," he said. "But that doesn't matter. I now know that heaven and hell exist. I have to warn people to change how they live and how they think, or they will end up where I was. If I can help one person avoid that, then I've done what God asked me to do."

Since spending time in hell, Ron has become committed to his faith and more involved at his church. He reads his Bible with enthusiasm. He tells his story often to anyone who will listen. Ron doesn't worry about the small stuff the way he once did. He confesses that he used to struggle with lust, but his old habits are simply gone now. He is less judgmental and less uptight about money. He knows God will provide.

After his close call with an eternity of torment, Ron's theology is very simple:

It matters how we live, but just being a good person is not enough.
We must confess our sinfulness to God and ask for forgiveness.
We are expected to pass on to others the love and forgiveness we have received.

"I know now my life on this planet is very short, but I'm not afraid of death anymore," he said. "I know God is real and that Jesus died so I don't have to go back to hell ever again."

4

Road Trip to
Redemption

— ✳ —

A serious accident gave Peter Bower a glimpse of
the afterlife—and the desire not to leave.

The shadows were starting to lengthen across Alton, Illinois, as a hot,
sticky afternoon in the summer of 1994 began its metamorphosis into
a pleasantly warm evening. Alton sprawls eastward from the banks of
the Mississippi River, just a stone's throw from where it is joined by
the Missouri in the long journey to the Gulf of Mexico.

The town is home to Southern Illinois University, where twenty-
six-year-old Peter Bower had just completed his second year of dental
school. As sunset approached that day, he had every reason to think
his life was *very* good. He had successfully completed national board
exams a few days earlier—a major milestone on the road to realizing his
dream of becoming a dentist. He had managed to get that far without

relying on his family for financial support, an accomplishment he was proud of. And he was heading home to spend an entire month with his parents at their home in Downs, a small town on the outskirts of Bloomington, Illinois. Life was good.

As Peter slid into the driver's seat of his tiny white and black Honda CRX for the trip, he especially looked forward to spending time working beside his dad, who was presently up to his ears in renovating the family home. The thought of hanging drywall or working on the roof for a few weeks was an appealing contrast to the stressful intellectual demands of school.

Nearly two and a half hours later, Peter exited Interstate 55 onto a two-lane county highway for the last leg of his journey—a route he'd traveled many times before. The road cut through gently rolling farmland that was covered in every direction by fields of shoulder-high corn. The sun had set at last, and away from the glare of the busy interstate the night was dark. Cool, moist air settled in the newly irrigated fields. Peter accelerated to feel the refreshing wind on his face through the open window—and to reach his destination a little sooner. Signs warned of road construction ahead, but he wasn't worried; he knew the road like the back of his hand. Besides, work was surely finished for the day. The posted speed limit was forty-five. He was doing fifty, maybe a little more.

About a mile from home, Peter crested the top of a gentle rise in the road. What he saw in his headlights on the other side made him instinctively cry out:

"Lord, help me!"

Peter Bower grew up in a Christian home. He was the youngest of five boys, with one sister, Becky, a year younger than Peter.

"We were a very close family," Peter recalled. "For most of my childhood, we lived in a small rural community in New York. We were poor but happy. My brothers and I would spend hours and hours in the woods pretty much doing whatever we wanted. There was always food on the table, but sometimes it came only from the garden because we had no money."

The family attended the Alliance Bible Church. At age three, Peter knew he wanted to become a believer too, and as he grew older, his faith became the focal point of his life. He was baptized during his senior year of high school.

In college, Peter helped establish a chapter of InterVarsity Christian Fellowship on campus. He developed a reputation as the guy who would openly speak up anytime the subject of evolution arose—which it frequently did in his many biology and anatomy classes. All a professor had to do was mention Darwinism, and his classmates would roll their eyes, put down their pens, and turn their attention toward Peter, knowing he would not pass up an opportunity to debate God's role as the sole Creator of the universe.

"I seemed to be going against the grain most of the time," Peter said. "I would go home almost every weekend, because nearly all my classmates were getting drunk or hanging out doing the things I wasn't interested in doing."

The words flew out of his mouth faster than thought: "Lord, help me!"

In the road, not more than a hundred feet ahead, stood a mound of dirt and sand left by the road construction crew. It was at least fifteen feet high and spilled into both lanes. Peter was driving too fast to avoid a collision. His car struck the shoulder of the pile and began to roll.

Not that Peter really noticed.

"As soon as those words passed my lips, a feeling came over me that is nearly impossible to describe," Peter remembered. "As my car rolled, it all seemed like a distant dream. In fact, I don't remember the events at all. What I do recall was the *feeling*—like being wrapped in a blanket of peace and love. I could not have cared less what was happening around me."

Peter had grown up hearing about the peace of God that "transcends understanding."[1] He even thought he had felt it once or twice in his life. Now as he flew through the air not wearing a seatbelt—and only vaguely aware of any danger—he experienced real peace for the first time.

"I think the reason I don't remember everything is because it didn't matter," Peter said. "Something far greater was happening—being held in that pervasive peace. I knew I wanted to stay right there forever, like it was the thing I'd been looking for all my life and didn't even know it. I was now complete."

Peter didn't feel his car come to rest. He has no memory of being ejected from the car as it rolled or of crawling from the wreckage. The next thing he knew, however, he was lying in the dirt in a cornfield beside the road. He felt no pain. His eyes were closed, yet he had a vivid sense of clarity and awareness. Peter has no idea how long he lay there, as time seemed to disappear. In that state, he felt an overwhelming sense of joy and peace.

"I was suddenly part of a vast culture of knowing, where nothing is hidden and everything is clear, so that fear and worry just vanish. Communication was naturally forming in my mind all the time. Words were completely irrelevant."

In this altered state of awareness, Peter intuitively knew two things. First, he didn't *ever* want to leave. Having arrived in such an indescribably beautiful place—far beyond anything he'd ever experienced on earth—he was determined to stay forever.

Second, he knew he *had* to leave. His glimpse of existence beyond this life was only temporary.

"I knew I had to go back, but I was putting up a fight," Peter said. "I didn't want to go. Then, for the first time I felt an actual being coming near me. I sensed it was an angel—a messenger—and it was there because I was resisting going back."

Peter could not see the being, but clearly perceived his powerful presence. When he spoke, Peter heard the words plainly—and audibly: "Your work isn't finished."

"He spoke with such undeniable authority," Peter recalled. "I knew I had to comply."

Becky Bower, age twenty-five, was alone in her parents' home that evening. She expected her brother Peter to arrive from school at any moment. Outside, the family dogs were frantically barking. In fact, Becky suddenly realized that they had been riled up for a while—at least half an hour. It was not like them to bark for so long. She stopped what she was doing and went to the window to investigate. Looking out, she wasn't really surprised to see Peter's car in front of the house.

But something was wrong. Even in the dark she could see the windshield was shattered and pushed in to within a few inches of the steering wheel. The roof was bent and buckled. Becky ran outside and found her brother lying on the ground beside the car. He seemed stunned and confused. She led him into the house, then called her parents on the phone and told them to come right away.

"I have no idea how I got home that night," Peter said. "One minute I was in the cornfield, the next minute Becky was helping me up off the ground in front of the house. I was really confused about where I was, but not *who* I was or what had just happened to me. It's part of the miracle how I got from one place to the other—I just don't know."

As Peter lay down on the couch in the living room, the incredible envelope of peace and love that surrounded him began to fade. Waiting for his parents to arrive, he felt increasingly disoriented and distressed.

"As that beautiful, peaceful feeling left me, another feeling took its place," Peter said. "But this time, it was a feeling of horrible guilt. I felt keenly aware of my own sin, and I felt shame and horror. My sins surrounded me now, instead of the peace I had felt only minutes earlier."

When his father arrived, Peter told him what had just happened—and of his feelings of deep unworthiness.

"He did what we always did in our family when a crisis came along," Peter recounted. "He prayed with me. I had been living a Christian life, but right then I asked Jesus to forgive me and to be my Lord. That made me feel better."

Apart from the mild concussion Peter suffered that night, there was not a scratch or a bruise anywhere on his body. But he was not the same man as before. He now knows firsthand what the "peace that transcends understanding" really feels like, and that it awaits him again someday. He also gained personal insight into how the prophet Isaiah felt when he saw God in a vision: "Woe to me! . . . I am ruined! For I am a man of unclean lips, and I live among a people of unclean lips."[2]

"I've lost all fear of death," said Peter, who has been a dentist for more than ten years and lives in Phoenix, Arizona. "I know for a fact that what lies on the other side is absolutely astounding. I know who I am and what's going to happen to me when I die. Most of all, I know we are truly saved by divine grace, and nothing else."

5

Upward and Onward

———— ✳ ————

Having questions about God, Marisa Vallbona
found answers through a near-fatal accident.

Nineteen-year-old Marisa Vallbona waited impatiently for her sister, Maria, in the living room of their parents' home in Houston, Texas. The two girls had plans to go for a run together, and Marisa was eager to get started. The noontime summer heat outside grew more intense by the minute. Marisa leaned over and retied the laces of her running shoes. She methodically stretched her hamstrings and other leg muscles—again. She put a cassette in her Walkman and placed the headphones over her ears.

Marisa wasn't a very tolerant person, and she didn't like to be kept waiting.

When Maria finally appeared, Marisa threw open the front door and charged into the glaring sunlight. The Gulf Coast heat swept over her like a molten avalanche. It would be a tough run today, but Marisa remained undeterred. It was in her nature—and a part of her upbringing—never to quit or take no for an answer. Besides, running time was Marisa's prayer time—and she had a *lot* on her mind that day. Since starting college a year ago, her life had been one long chain of vexing questions. Today she planned to talk to God until he came through with some solid answers.

She cranked the volume on her Walkman and ran. After only a couple of blocks, her white shorts and shirt were already soaked, and her blond hair was slick with sweat. She labored to breathe in the dense, humid air. Still, she pressed forward. Ten minutes later, Maria signaled that she'd had enough and was turning back. Marisa nodded—and went on without her. Her prayerful purpose that day was too important to abandon so soon.

Marisa was raised in the Catholic Church, but she'd been a misfit and a rebel from the very beginning. Her Spanish father, a renowned physician and sought-after lecturer, took her with him on his many business trips abroad.

"Everywhere we went, he'd drag me to Mass," Marisa said.

And she didn't like it. She was not drawn in by the pomp and ceremony and liturgies.

When it came time for Marisa, at age seven, to receive her First Communion in the church, she dutifully attended catechism classes. She met every requirement put before her—except one: She refused to go to confession. Marisa told the nuns in charge of her education that she didn't believe it was right to confess her sins to a mere person. She would confess directly to God or not at all.

Full of spunk even then, she challenged the nuns to read their Bibles more closely if they didn't believe her. Eventually they conceded and allowed her to take Communion without going to confession.

At age twelve, Marisa attended a Baptist summer camp. The

Protestant emphasis on an intimate, personal relationship with God, based on grace, was different from the Catholic approach she'd been taught—and it appealed to her immensely. Back at school, she became actively involved in Young Life, a campus ministry that reaches out to teenagers. Throughout high school, Marisa's relationship with God continued to mature and deepen. Her faith had become unshakable.

Or so she thought.

After her graduation in 1982, Marisa enrolled in a prominent liberal university, where she was immersed in an entirely different philosophical worldview than the one she had known. On campus, God seemed to have been banished from every classroom and dormitory. Everywhere she turned, she was confronted by Darwinistic thinking and a deeply entrenched belief in science and reason as the only possible source of ultimate truth. Predictably, she began to question her faith in the face of so much competing and contradictory "evidence."

As if that weren't enough, nearly all her newfound friends seemed to be having a great time—drinking, doing drugs, and having sex. Aside from trying alcohol like nearly everyone, Marisa didn't follow along with the "party" crowd. She and her boyfriend decided to avoid sex and even attended church together. But being surrounded by so many contradictory influences was enough to make her question her own view of right and wrong.

"I'd always tried to walk straight," she said, "but the way these people were living suddenly looked like so much *fun*. I asked God, 'Am I wrong to be tempted? Why do I feel like I'm growing apart from you? What's the right thing to do?'"

These were the questions swirling through Marisa's mind as she ran that day, the sticky asphalt radiating heat like a hot griddle beneath her pounding feet. She turned onto a street that led past the neighborhood swimming pool, where she had spent many hours as a teenager. The cool, refreshing water had never looked more inviting—but she would not stop. She was driven by a single question forming in her mind, one that summed up all the others that troubled her:

"God, are you truly real?"

According to those who witnessed what happened next, Marisa should not be alive today. She should have died—and not come back.

A huge early 1980s-model Cadillac rounded the corner behind Marisa. A big-boned blonde in her forties named Diane was at the wheel. It remains a mystery why she didn't see Marisa running on the road ahead, a few feet from the curb. Maybe her eyes were drawn toward the swimming pool that was packed with people that day. Maybe she was adjusting the car's air-conditioner, or switching channels on the radio. Maybe Marisa wandered into her path, distracted by the music playing in her ears and the questions troubling her mind. Whatever the reason, Diane hit Marisa directly from behind.

Wham!

The impact tossed the girl's body into the air like a rag doll. She came down hard on the hood of the car, with the sickening *whump* of buckling metal. Reflexively, Diane slammed on the brakes. Marisa rolled off the hood and fell limply to the pavement beside the car. It finally came to a stop, with the rear wheel pinning Marisa's right leg to the ground.

The whole catastrophe unfolded in less than two seconds.

The on-duty lifeguard across the street watched it all in horrifying slow motion from his umbrella-covered perch overlooking the pool. He was Marisa's age, a former high school classmate of hers named Smokey Mountain. He ran faster than he'd ever run to the scene of the accident and performed mouth-to-mouth resuscitation. Marisa was unconscious and blood poured from a cut on her head. He ran back to the pool office and dialed 9-1-1.

Mercifully, Marisa—that is, the part of her that was conscious and aware—was not present for any of the above. She never realized she was about to be hit by a car. She didn't feel it strike the back of her legs. She had no sensation of being hurled into the air, landing on the hood of the car, or falling to the asphalt.

"I immediately left my body," she recalled. "One minute I was running, the next minute I felt like I was on the outside of everyday life. It was dark. I don't mean creepy dark, just dark like having your eyes closed. I couldn't see anything, but I knew God was very, very present. I felt really, really good."

Marisa struggles, like so many people who've had similar experiences, to find the right words to describe what happened to her. Language, she says, can only crudely approximate the ineffable quality of the sensations she felt and the radically altered state of awareness she enjoyed while outside of her body.

"To have some idea, get in the deep end of a swimming pool," Marisa said. "Go under the water and hear how quiet it is—experience how peaceful you feel just floating there. Open your eyes and you can see all these other bodies swimming along beside you. You are suddenly aware of things you couldn't see a moment ago, because they were hidden underwater. Your movements are effortless. Nothing hurts. You don't even feel gravity or the weight of your body. You have no wants, no needs, no fears."

As soon as she left her body, Marisa was filled with a deep, indescribable feeling of peace and well-being. She knew she had died and wondered why she had ever been so afraid of something so wonderful. Knowledge and communication were fundamentally different from anything she'd ever experienced in life. Nothing was hidden from her mind. She had only to think a question to know its answer.

Marisa became aware of other beings all around her on a "spiritual plane." She doesn't know if they were angels or human spirits. But they were each made of a beautiful, radiant light. None were threatening or frightening in appearance. She remembers feeling astonished to realize that living people are surrounded by such a rich spiritual reality all the time—and are completely oblivious to it. She had been a Christian for several years but had never been taught just how close the spiritual plane really is.

"I felt perfectly safe and at home," Marisa said. "And I had the sensation of moving upward through the darkness toward something; I never saw what. I didn't go toward a bright light like some people describe. But I definitely felt like I was moving up."

As she traveled, Marisa began to think that she wasn't ready to die.

"I thought, *I'm only nineteen. I'd like to see how my life turns out, to see if I succeed in life and if I have kids.* Right then, I felt that I was a participant in the decision, like it was my choice."

Then Marisa had a conversation with God.

"I said to him, 'Now that I know what death is all about and that it is totally cool, send me back and let's see what kind of a difference I can make. I'm going to sing your praises and spread the Word. Put me to work!'"

God told Marisa, "I will send you back, and you will make a difference—now that you know I am *real.*"

Then Marisa stopped moving upward and away from her earthly life. She was suddenly hovering in the air above the scene of her accident. She could see what was happening below with startling clarity. She saw her body on the ground covered in blood. Paramedics had arrived and were preparing to place her in an ambulance. Her mother and sister stood at the back of the ambulance, sobbing and screaming. A large crowd of onlookers from the swimming pool stood in a wide circle in the street around her lifeless body. Marisa felt no fear or pain at what she saw, but took it all in as if it were happening to someone else.

In a flash, that feeling of detachment came to an abrupt halt.

"I was right back in my body," she said. "The pain was instantly excruciating. Even worse was the feeling of not belonging here anymore."

Marisa suffered a concussion that day and a nasty gash on her head. She was bruised and scratched up, but no bones were broken—not even the leg that wound up under the car's wheel. However, to this day she suffers from severe migraine headaches that began after the accident.

But Marisa was undoubtedly changed dramatically by her near-death experience. She became much less judgmental and more focused on looking for the good in people. Though she has enjoyed a successful career, achievement and accolades in life took a backseat to serving God. She has never felt the slightest fear of death. On the contrary, she looks forward to it when her time does come. Most important of all, she has never again questioned her faith—and she isn't shy about sharing it with others.

"I know with absolute certainty that God exists," she said. "We are accountable to him, and we would be crazy not to believe in him and have a relationship with him. Now I know we can die at any given moment. You don't have until tomorrow. When it comes to getting your faith in order, *right now* is all you've got."

On some days, Marisa, who now lives in La Jolla, California, wishes she had not asked to come back to earth. Then she thinks of her two wonderful sons and she remembers why she did: to "make a difference" for them—and anyone else willing to listen to her story.

PART TWO

Someone to Watch Over Me

Angels, wearing halos or Harley jackets, regularly intervene in the lives of ordinary people.

Have you noticed the increase in angel sightings over the past decade? We're not talking about *actual* angelic encounters—though we can't rule that out. We mean our society's fascination with these heaven-sent beings. They seem to be everywhere these days: blogs and bumper stickers, trinkets and TV shows, music videos, and coffee mugs.

Not that long ago, the popularity of angels saw a dramatic spike around Christmastime. We would all sing familiar carols such as "Angels We Have Heard on High" and "Hark! the Herald Angels Sing." Millions tuned in annually to watch the holiday film classic *It's a Wonderful Life*, with George Bailey and his kind but clumsy guardian angel, Clarence Odbody. And many of us grew up listening to Mom or Dad read the nativity story from the New Testament, in which angels played a starring role: "Greetings, you who are highly favored!" an angel tells Mary. "You will be with child and give birth to a son, and you are to give him the name Jesus" (Luke 1:28, 31).

More recently, the interest in angels has gained momentum and is not only the domain of holiday hoopla. Who can forget the popular TV show *Touched by an Angel* that aired from 1994 to 2003? It was a feel-good series that featured a group of angels sent by God to help humans mired in a mess of one sort or another.

And today your search for angelic insights will reap a bounty of material, some genuinely helpful, most of it not so much. There are thousands of CDs, videos, Web sites, novels, seminars, and retreats ready to aid your quest for angelic intervention. More than a few books promise to show you how to "activate" angels in your life.

All of this interest in angels is good in the sense that it opens people's hearts and minds to the awareness of the spiritual world and the participation of God's emissaries in our daily lives. The downside is that much of the information being dispensed is based not on fact but on fantasy and fabrication (much of which we discussed in *Heaven and the Afterlife*). With that in mind, here's a biblically based version of "Angels 101"[1]:

The term itself comes from the Greek *angelos*, which means "messenger." In ancient times, when travel was slow and communication limited, personally delivered messages were coveted and critical; battles could be won or lost due to a courier's expedience or delay. It's not surprising that Greek mythology has a winged messenger as one of its gods: Hermes—also known as Mercury in later Roman times. Other cultures and religions included the idea of messenger gods. And then there is Hebrew literature, which contains many accounts of angelic messengers with names like Michael and Gabriel.

Scripture provides these angelic insights for us:

First, angels, like humans, are creatures, meaning "God-*created*." They are not equal to God, but exist to carry out his missions and accomplish his will.

Second, they have personality—intellect (thought), emotion (feeling), and will (choice). They are creatures with distinct and unique abilities, purposes, and personalities.

Third, they exist in time and space. They're limited by these dimensions, although they have much more freedom than we do. The writer of the book of Psalms says the angels should praise God because he created them.[2] Another song of praise says humans were made "a little lower than the heavenly beings."[3] Like us, angels are personal creatures: responsible, accountable, and dependent upon God.

Though existing in time and space, angels seem able to appear and disappear suddenly or travel from one place to another very quickly. They often appear in some kind of glorified humanlike form—with unusual brightness resembling fire, lightning, polished metal or precious stones, and/or shining white linen clothing.[4] Other angels, not resembling humans at all, are likened to unusual beasts.[5]

There's no question angels are superhuman. The angel encountered by the Old Testament prophet Daniel was stronger, smarter, and faster than any human. He could fight heavenly battles, see into the future, and even though it took time, go between Persia and Babylon without breaking a sweat. But they aren't all-powerful or all-knowing, and they cannot be everywhere at once. Only God has these qualities.

With that basic knowledge in mind, it's also safe to say that we don't know when angels might appear and, if they do, in what form. As protectors, they are unpredictable. As messengers, they are mysterious. They do God's bidding, and frankly, we don't always understand what God's bidding is. Theologian F. Forrester Church wrote:

If angels came in packages, we'd almost always pick the wrong one. Even as the devil is evil disguised as good, angels are goodness disguised. They show up in foolscap, calico, gingham, and brown paper bags. Jesus discovered the realm of God in a mustard seed, the smallest and least portentous of all seeds. Mustards seeds and angels have this in common. They are little epiphanies of the divine amidst the ordinary.[6]

Despite what we don't know about angels, surely there's one thing we do know: they are at this moment actively engaged in the affairs of our world and our individual lives. They are helping, guiding, protecting—usually unseen.

When we share stories of angelic encounters—like ones in the pages ahead—many people wonder, "Why didn't angels come to my rescue when I needed them? Where were they in my time of trouble?" The obvious answer is: God only knows. But there's another answer, just as true: It's highly likely that angels have swooped into your life at various times unnoticed or unrecognized. Who knows how many times you've been shielded from evil forces? Who knows how many times you've been saved from a fatal accident by a hairsbreadth? Who knows how many times a blessing has dropped in your lap "coincidentally"? You'll never know—this side of heaven.

Yet another thing is true: We probably rub shoulders with angels much more than we realize. As the writer of Hebrews advised: "Do not forget to entertain strangers, for by so doing some people have entertained angels without knowing it."[7] If you doubt for a moment that angels show up at unexpected times, in unexpected ways, just read the stories to follow and see if your faith in God's messengers isn't bolstered.

6

Angels All Around

——— ✳ ———

On the brink of death, Ryan Heer brought
home a message from beyond.

The medical student stood for several minutes studying the face of the
little boy in the bed in front of her. Turning to his mother, she asked,
"Do you have a picture of him?"

Cheryl Heer glanced over at her five-year-old son. He was unconscious, his neck, face, and head swollen to twice its normal size. She
couldn't see his eyes or, for that matter, any other features that made
him recognizable as the vivacious little boy he was. Cheryl walked
numbly to her purse and pulled a school photo from her wallet.

An ICU nurse herself, Cheryl knew exactly what the med student
was thinking and why she needed the photo. The nurse was thinking,
I can't see a kid in there.

Cheryl had done the same thing at times, asking families for photographs of her patients. Caregivers asked for photos when patients were so ill or wounded they were barely recognizable as human beings. It helped the nursing staff reconnect and remember that this was a real person they were treating.

That's when Cheryl realized the gravity of the situation.

It was hard to believe that one week earlier Ryan was at home with his younger brother, Jordan, watching cartoons and eating popsicles while the two boys recovered from routine cases of chicken pox. When one large pock behind Ryan's ear turned red and began to swell, Cheryl and her husband, Jeff, weren't too worried. But as the swelling continued, they realized something was terribly wrong. Within hours, Ryan's neck had swollen so much that it pushed his head over against his left shoulder. What's more, his temperature shot up to 105 degrees.

Rushed by ambulance to Riley Hospital for Children in Indianapolis, Ryan's condition only worsened. His head, swollen to twice its normal size, had been pushed upright again because the massive swelling had spread now to both sides of his neck. His temperature remained elevated, and his torso grew inflamed and red. As infection raged throughout his body, he was put on oxygen and a heart monitor in anticipation of pneumonia or cardiac arrest.

The infection was being caused by streptococcus bacteria that had invaded one of Ryan's chicken pox. At that point, the swelling had so severely twisted Ryan's neck that doctors were afraid it would break and damage his spinal column. Believing the infection had entered Ryan's bones, doctors wanted to operate so they could scrape the infection from Ryan's vertebrae and insert pins to hold everything together. Still, they were certain Ryan would not survive the surgery. They also knew he would not survive without surgery. Concluding there was nothing left to do but wait, they fully expected Ryan to die from a broken neck.

On a Sunday evening ten days after their ordeal began, Jeff was at home with two-year-old Jordan. Alone with Ryan in his hospital room, Cheryl wept over the realization that her son was dying.

There had been another Ryan, years ago, but he'd died too. Ryan Updyke wasn't actually Cheryl's brother, but he might as well have been. The little boy had been just three years old—and Cheryl seven—when he became part of her family. The son of Cheryl's mother's best friend—a single mom who worked evenings—Ryan spent most afternoons and evenings at Cheryl's home. When he was sixteen, Ryan was diagnosed with bone cancer. He died eighteen months later. When Cheryl and Jeff married and had their first baby, they named him after the "little brother" Cheryl had loved and lost.

Cheryl's son didn't know about the young man whose name he shared. She had been looking forward to telling him about the older Ryan one day. Now it seemed that day would never come. As Cheryl looked around Ryan's room—overflowing with hundreds of cards, stuffed animals, and flowers—she knew that people in churches all over the country were praying for Ryan. And yet it felt like hope was draining away with every passing hour.

Cheryl saw Jeff's devotional Bible lying open on a nearby table. Picking it up, she read a reflection written by Billy Graham about Psalm 91:11: "For he will command his angels concerning you to guard you in all your ways."

Could God send angels to guard Ryan? Where would he put them? Cheryl looked around Ryan's room again. It was definitely standing-room only. Too many stuffed animals and balloons, not to mention all the medical equipment. The only empty places in the room were the corners. Sobbing, she began to pray.

Through her tears, she prayed, "Lord, send four of your angels to guard the four corners of this room. Watch over my son, protect him, comfort him if he's in any pain, and guide him home to you if he's not going to stay here with us."

Cheryl soon fell into a troubled sleep, waking every few minutes to the sounds of beepers and monitors, and the bustle of nurses coming and going throughout the night.

At the Heer family home, Jeff was praying a different kind of prayer. Having finally gotten Jordan to bed, Jeff paced the house. Finally, in his bathrobe, he went into the backyard and looked up at the stars. Raising his arms, he yelled toward the heavens, "What's going to happen? God, help us!"

The following night, it was Cheryl's turn to stay home with Jordan while Jeff spent the night by Ryan's side.

The last thing Cheryl did before falling into an exhausted sleep was to phone the room and speak with Jeff.

"How is he?" she asked, then listened as he told her there was no change and that Ryan was still unconscious but appeared to be resting well.

Cheryl went to sleep. Ever since she'd read Billy Graham's devotional, she'd had a sense of peace. No matter what happened, God was going to see them through this devastating trial.

The next morning, Cheryl phoned Jeff again. She could hardly utter the words "Good morning" before her husband said, "You need to get down here right away."

Cheryl's heart dropped into her heels. In a panic, she choked out the words, "Why? What's happened?"

"Because Ryan woke up around four this morning and started crawling around his bed, rearranging all his pillows. He said they weren't comfortable enough!" Jeff laughed. "Just get here as quick as you can!"

When Cheryl walked into Ryan's hospital room, he opened his eyes—mere slits in his still-swollen face—and called out, "Hi, Mommy!"

An influx of doctors and nurses kept Ryan busy for hours. At one point, Ryan's doctor turned to Jeff and Cheryl and said, "Well, things are turning around. Thank God we didn't take him into surgery! Let's just see how he does."

Ryan's swelling continued to subside by the hour.

Later that day, Ryan's grandmother pulled him in a little red wagon to the hospital library to watch a movie. The following day, he colored Easter eggs and got to sit in the wagon again while Cheryl pulled him to the nurse's station so he could tell her where to hide the eggs.

Two days later, he was home.

Ryan spent the next several days lying on the couch and watching cartoons and movies. He was still weak, but recovering quickly.

One day when he'd been home about a week, Cheryl was sitting at her dressing table putting on makeup while Ryan sat on a little bench next to her table and watched and played, as he often did.

Cheryl said, "Ryan, you were so, so sick!"

They talked about his stay in the hospital. She was thankful he remembered nothing from the first ten days when he was either in excruciating pain or unconscious.

"I remember the wagon," Ryan told her as he played with some string he'd pulled out of his pocket. "And seeing a movie. And coloring eggs."

"I prayed for you, Ryan," his mother said. "I prayed for angels to watch over you and help you not feel bad."

"Yeah, I know," he answered.

She looked at him quizzically. "What do you mean, *you know?*"

"I know," he said. "I saw the angels."

Cheryl glanced at her son. Now he was playing with her makeup brushes. "Really? Where were the angels, Ryan? What did they look like?"

Ryan said matter-of-factly, "They were standing in the corners of the room. And flying around too. There were mommy and daddy ones, and baby ones and grandma and grandpa ones. They were yellow and white and really pretty."

Cheryl didn't know what to think. She half-believed him. Then again, maybe through his coma he'd heard her praying.

"I had a dream too," Ryan said as he hopped around the table.

73

"About Jesus. We were planting stuff in a garden. He said I was a good boy and that he loved me."

She looked at her son in wonder. "That's interesting. Anything else?"

Ryan was getting fidgety now. He'd sat for too long and was ready to play. He started skipping toward the door. Cheryl turned back to her mirror.

But he stopped and said over his shoulder, "Oh, yeah. Ryan says '*Hi.*'"

Something pierced Cheryl's heart. She turned toward him. "Wait. Come back here. What did you say?"

Ryan skipped back to the dressing table.

Cheryl stared at her son. "What did you say?"

"Ryan said to tell you '*Hi.*'"

"Anything else?"

"Nope." And he skipped off.

Cheryl sat there for a long time, crying. So it was true. Everything her son had seen and told her was true. God had answered Jeff's prayer for help, and Cheryl's prayers for angels, then sent her a message from the older Ryan too, so she would believe. Her heart overflowed with gratitude.

A week later the phone rang. It was one of the coaches with the T-ball league at the local YMCA saying that Ryan would be on his team. Jeff and Cheryl had signed Ryan up to play T-ball months ago, before his razor-thin brush with death. Cheryl explained everything to the coach, adding, "He's still getting his strength back, but I know he really wants to play. Why don't we bring him to practices and see how he does?"

Ryan did great, playing first base all spring and summer—and the next summer, and the summer after that—eventually playing baseball through junior high.

Not that it should have come as any surprise considering the name of Ryan's very first T-ball team: the Angels.

7

Divine Defenders

— ✳ —

Martha Cabot and her granddaughter, Abby,
know from firsthand experience that angels are
real—and ready to lend a hand when
we need them most.

In late June 2004, Martha Cabot and her seven-year-old granddaughter, Abby, stepped out of an air-conditioned movie theater in Fort Worth, Texas, into a hot and muggy summer evening. The sun had just disappeared below the horizon, and a murky dusk was quickly turning to night. The two were laughing and discussing the animated film they'd just seen. To Martha, the sound of Abby's laughter was like sweet music; it had been some time since she'd heard it.

Abby's father, Robert—Martha's son—had been called to active duty, along with the rest of his National Guard field hospital unit, and sent to Iraq for fifteen months. He'd been gone for five months already, but to everyone in the family it felt more like five years. In addition to the emotional burden of constant worry for Robert's safety, the family was under heavy financial pressure, since his military paycheck did not fully cover monthly expenses. Abby's mother, Rachel, had been forced to take a second job. Most of all, the strain of Robert's absence was taking a toll on Abby. With every passing day she grew more withdrawn and sullen.

Martha had recently decided she wasn't going to let fear and uncertainty defeat her family without a fight. She had just emerged from a lengthy battle with depression after the sudden death of her husband in a car crash two years earlier. The turning point in her own recovery had arrived when she resolved to keep busy with things she enjoyed, no matter how bad she might feel on any given day. Martha would invoke the same wisdom to help Abby—with tickets to the ballet, regular ice-cream dates to try out new flavors, trips to the zoo or the children's museum—anything to remind them both that the world was still a safe, fun place to be, even when hardships arise.

It had been an especially hard week for everyone, and Martha found herself looking forward to a little childlike frivolity. Today, Abby had chosen to go see the latest Disney film—just the thing they needed: a good dose of singing and silliness. After the movie was over, the theater emptied out quickly, but Martha and Abby lingered until the credits ended. By the time they gathered their things and emerged through the exit into the parking lot, the rest of the moviegoers had already found their cars and driven away.

"Holding Abby's hand as we walked and laughed together felt really, really good," Martha said later. "It was like we were the only two people in the world that day, and nothing could possibly harm us. Our troubles seemed very far away."

But that feeling didn't last long. They had walked half the distance to the car when Martha sensed movement in her peripheral vision. She looked and saw four young men walking across the nearly empty parking lot—on a course to intercept them. The man leading the others was tall and slender. He wore an oversized sports jersey and baggy pants that were barely held up by a belt that rode beneath his hips. A ball cap sat sideways on his head. As he walked, he never took his eyes off of Martha. The others behind him stole furtive glances at her as well, when they weren't scanning the parking lot for signs that someone might be watching.

Martha knew instantly they were in trouble. She glanced back toward the theater, judging how long it would take to reach the safety of the lobby. An icy panic flooded her body when she saw a fifth young man following them—and blocking their retreat. Martha tightened her grip on Abby's hand and quickened her step toward the car. The leader of the gang matched her accelerated pace and stepped between her and the driver-side door just before she reached it. Up close, Martha saw that he wasn't a man at all, but a teenage boy of about seventeen. His arms were covered in menacing tattoos, and his eyes were hard and determined. His body may be young, Martha realized, but that doesn't make him less dangerous.

"What do you want?" she asked, with more confidence than she felt.

The young man grinned. "We're taking donations for our college fund today," he said. "You want to help us get a head start in life, don't you?"

The rest of the gang now stood in a loose circle around Martha and Abby. Someone snickered at the dark humor.

"I'd love to help you," Martha said, her voice trembling with tension, "but threatening an old woman and a little girl is hardly what I'd call a head start in life."

"Thanks for the tip," he said, his face hardening with malice. "Now give me your purse." He looked at Abby, clutching her grandmother's arm with one hand and the child's purse she'd received for her last birthday in the other. "You too, runt."

Martha scanned the area, desperately hoping to see someone who might hear a call for help. Night had deepened now, so that all she saw were cones of light thrown by street lamps onto the now empty parking lot. Traffic streamed by on an adjacent road–too far away to offer any hope. She knew they were on their own.

"Do it now!" the young man shouted and stepped closer to Martha, towering above her menacingly. The others moved inward as well.

Martha's split-second reaction surprised her. Instead of feeling frightened and helpless–as the gang clearly intended–she was flooded with courage she couldn't explain. She thought of her son serving in the desert halfway around the world, doing his part to rid the world of terrorism. She wasn't about to give in to it so easily here at home. And alongside that resolve, she felt a deep, inexplicable compassion for these boys who had lost their way so completely.

Martha tightened her grip on her purse and on Abby's hand.

"No," she said, firmly. "We won't give you anything."

The young man's face twisted into a mask of anger. He spat out a string of vicious expletives and grabbed hold of Abby's purse. He yanked it so hard that she fell to the ground–still holding on to the purse strap. He drew back his foot to kick at her.

"Don't you dare!" Martha cried and reflexively bent down to shield her granddaughter.

One of the other men shoved her violently from behind. As she fell, someone ripped her purse from her shoulder. Martha braced herself on the pavement with both arms to keep from landing hard on Abby. She sat up with her back against the car door. She knew there was nothing else she could do to prevent the gang from finishing what they had started. The leader was ranting now about giving them "what they deserved."

"Dear God, have mercy," she said aloud and gathered Abby in her arms. "Lord, protect us."

"Ma'am, are you all right?"

The words rang out from several yards away in a deep, resonant voice. Martha strained to see who it was, but her view was blocked by the car.

"Help us!" she cried.

The gang leader, now fully enraged, shouted some more expletives then yelled back at the man, "It's none of your business! Get out of here!"

"No, I don't think we can do that," he said, stepping from behind the rear of the car. He was joined by a second man who stood calmly beside him. "Return what you've taken and leave. *Now.*"

"I was looking right at them," Martha recalled later, "but I couldn't see their features very well. All I can say is that they were big and gave off an incredibly comforting sense of power and confidence. It's like they were instantly in control of the situation."

Martha heard receding footsteps as some of the gang members ran away without a word. The leader hesitated. His back was turned to her, but Martha imagined him glaring at the two men, calculating his chances against them. A tense silence lasted a few seconds, and then he suddenly dropped Martha's purse and took off running as fast as he could go.

"Oh, thank you, God!" Martha said in deep relief. "Thank you! Thank you!" She got to her feet and helped Abby up.

Martha called out loudly to the men, "If you hadn't come along, I don't know what would have happened!"

But as Martha looked around, she was suddenly confused.

"Where did those men go?" Abby asked.

Martha saw no trace of their rescuers in any direction. She did see the gang leader disappear into the darkness at the edge of the lighted parking lot, still running as if his life depended on it—but no one was pursuing him. She and Abby were completely alone.

It was a mystery, but she wasn't going to stand around trying to solve it. Martha hurriedly loaded Abby in the car and drove straight home.

Later, however, after reflecting on the evening's events, she came to an inescapable conclusion: God had sent his angels to protect Abby and her from certain harm. From the moment the two "bodyguards" arrived, she had felt safe and secure, enveloped in a comforting presence that she could only describe as supernatural. It had been a wide, open area where they had been confronted by the thugs—and where the protectors had appeared—and surely she would've seen them walking away. In an instant, they had simply vanished from sight.

"When I tell this story, a lot of people want to speculate about what might have happened had the angels not intervened," Martha said. "But all I can think about is that they *did* help us, and what that means about our ability to trust in God's merciful protection."

Paradoxically, the incident served to strengthen the family's faith that Robert was being cared for too. At prayer times, Abby took to asking the angels, with unshakable conviction, to please watch over her daddy. Martha understood where the girl's new ability to trust had come from: She had seen God's angels with her own eyes. And indeed, Robert remained safe throughout his tour of duty.

8

Friends of the Family

—— ✳ ——

Stricken with cancer, teenager Carly Kilander
drew comfort from frequent visitors
not of this world.

On the fifth anniversary of her daughter's death, Kim Kilander worked late. Earlier in the week, co-workers had covered Kim's desk with so many cards and balloons that the day before a young woman from another department had stopped to ask Kim if it was her birthday.

After Kim explained that the flowers were to honor her daughter Carly, a flash of recognition crossed the face of the twenty-something woman standing before her.

"Your husband wrote a book about your daughter, didn't he?" she asked. "I've wanted to read it."

They chatted for a few minutes, and as her visitor walked away,

Kim couldn't help but notice she was about Carly's age. Or, to be more precise, the age Carly would have been if she were still alive.

It had lifted Kim's spirits being able to talk about her daughter with the young woman. But today, on the anniversary of Carly's death, Kim felt melancholy. Her daughter's passing had been as extraordinary as her life, but what difference did it make now, five years after the fact? Her family and friends had been through so much. Had it all been in vain?

The last two months of Carly's life had been filled with pain—but with miracles as well. Take, for example, the angels.

The first time they had showed up was on a Sunday. The day began oddly anyway because from the moment Carly woke up she was her old self. She felt bright and lucid, not groggy and pain-addled like she'd been for several weeks.

———

Carly was no stranger to pain. When she was just eighteen months old, she'd been diagnosed with neurofibromatosis, a disorder that causes large, benign tumors to grow in the nervous system. Other symptoms of the disorder include abnormal development of the spine, skull, and shin bone. Indeed, by the time Carly was thirteen, she'd undergone a dozen operations. One stubborn problem had been a severe bow in her ankle bones. Doctors had tried everything to remedy the problem, implanting bone chips from Carly's hip, a battery pack to stimulate growth, and finally a metal rod. But nothing seemed to help. Almost every night, Carly would ask her mom or dad to rub her foot, finding relief in their touch.

In December of her senior year in high school, Carly complained that she wasn't feeling well. One day in early February, she came home from school embarrassed because she had lost control of her bladder while in class. When a CT scan revealed a large tumor, doctors operated to remove it—plus her uterus, both ovaries, and four inches of colon. Unlike Carly's previous tumors, this one was not benign, and Carly underwent a second surgery in May, and began chemotherapy in June.

Before the end of the year, she had received five rounds of chemotherapy and was hospitalized five times.

In January hospice was called.

A few weeks later, the Kilanders' pastor visited Carly and prayed that angels would surround her. Perhaps his prayer brought the angels, or maybe the angels had been there all along. Either way, about a week after he prayed, they started showing up.

———

Carly woke up that Sunday morning "bright-eyed and bushy-tailed," as her dad, Scott, liked to call it. After Scott and Adam, Carly's fifteen-year-old brother, left for church, Kim carried her daughter from her bedroom to the family room. It wasn't all that daunting a task—at that point Carly weighed a hundred pounds, despite being five-feet-nine-inches tall.

After getting Carly settled comfortably in her favorite chair overlooking their sunny backyard, Kim asked, "Do you need anything? What can I get you?"

Carly shook her head happily. "Nothing. I'm good."

Kim headed to the bathroom. Two minutes later she heard Carly yell.

"Mom! Come quick!"

Kim ran back into the family room.

Carly beamed. "Mom, you missed it!"

Kim looked around. "What, sweetheart? What did I miss?"

"Sit down," her daughter instructed. When Kim complied, Carly took her hand and held it. "Mom, you missed the most beautiful light. For just a second, I thought the TV had come on by itself, but that wasn't it at all. I could *feel* the light. And I was looking at it, studying it, and then . . ."

Carly began to rub her mother's hand.

She continued breathlessly, "And then, Mom, I felt this—like I'm rubbing your hand. But on my foot. A soft hand rubbed the top of my foot. Just like this. Then a wave went through my body from my toes to my head. It was the most wonderful sensation, Mom. And it wasn't the meds. I know it wasn't the meds."

Kim asked, "Carly, do you know what it was?"

Carly smiled.

Kim answered her own question: "It was an angel."

"I know, Mom," Carly said.

When her dad walked in the door from church a couple of hours later, Carly made him sit down in front of her and then repeated the entire story.

Scott looked at Carly's right leg, riddled with scars of every size from so many surgeries. His eyes welled up.

"Which foot was it?" he asked, even though he was certain he already knew.

Carly said, "My right one."

The angels showed up regularly after that. Carly referred to them as her friends. They seemed to be of every age, many of them children.

One afternoon, Kim walked into Carly's bedroom and found her crying softly. Kim reached for her hand. "Sweetheart, why are you so sad?"

"The little boy was just here," Carly answered, "and he was packing up my things to go. Where am I going, Mom?"

Kim—knowing that her daughter was in pain and hated traveling anywhere—assured Carly there were no errands or doctors' visits planned that day. They would be staying home.

Later, when Kim told her best friend Carol about what Carly had seen, Carol said simply, "Kim, don't you realize what's happening? The Lord is preparing Carly to leave this world. He sent an angel to help her pack. He's preparing her mentally."

Tears filled Kim's eyes. "You're right, Carol." It was a bittersweet realization.

Carly often made comments like, "My friends are here," or "I saw my friends today."

Then one evening, she had an experience of a different kind— apparently, a visit from a deceased relative.

Carly looked at her mom and asked matter-of-factly, "Mom, did one of your aunts just die?"

Kim said, "No, why?"

The girl motioned with her eyes toward the kitchen. "She looks kind of like you, Mom, like she might be related to us."

Kim looked toward the kitchen, which appeared empty but apparently was not. "Are you sure it's not Great-Grammy?"

Carly rolled her eyes as only a teenager can do and said, "C'mon, Mom. I know what Great-Grammy looks like, and that's not her."

So it wasn't Scott's grandmother. Who else could it be? Kim thought for a moment, and then said, "You know what? I'll bet it's *my* grandmother. She died in a car accident when she was about my age."

"I think you're right, Mom," Carly answered.

Kim breathed a small sigh and felt comforted. Could it really be her grandmother watching over Carly? God had apparently given her permission to visit her descendants on earth.

That night Scott came home from his job at a nearby construction site. He spent time with Carly and helped Adam with schoolwork. Around nine-thirty or ten, as the household began to wind down toward bedtime, he went to the computer in the living room.

When Carly's battle with cancer began the previous year, Scott hardly knew how to turn on a computer. But with so many family members and friends praying for Carly, it had been important to keep everyone informed. Carly had started keeping a journal at a Web site called *caringbridge.com*, where families facing health crises can post updates and communicate with friends and family. As Carly weakened, Scott started logging regular updates, always typing with two fingers. Carly's bedroom was around the corner from the computer desk, and she would answer her dad's questions so he could share her thoughts in their online journal. Sometimes, as Scott wrote, Kim would be lying on the couch next to him, crying softly into the cushions.

Indeed, Carly's suffering was immense. Her bowels would clog several times a day, and the bile would churn in her stomach until she threw up. She dwindled to ninety pounds. She was smart, and she knew what was happening to her, but she never got mad. Just gracious and grateful–grateful for her family, friends, and the gift of her angels.

One day Kim told Scott, "I wish I could see what Carly sees. At the same time, it feels like such a personal, intimate thing between Carly and God. So whether I see Carly's friends or not, I'm just thankful God is taking care of her."

Scott understood. As a young man, he'd had the amazing experience of seeing angels surrounding the pulpit at his church. Another time, he'd picked up a hitchhiker who had disappeared suddenly after asking to be dropped off in an empty parking lot. Scott was pretty sure the young man had been an angel.

For Scott, Carly's angels were more than a window into the afterlife. He told a friend, "Carly's angels have given me a trust in God that nothing can take away. Nothing worse than what I've gone through can happen to me. Watching my little girl suffer the way she did took me to the bottom, to the pit, to hell and back. And God was with us even there."

Carly died on March 16, 2004, surrounded by Kim, Scott, Adam, her aunt Chris, and of course, her angel friends.

And yet her story didn't end with her death.

For a year after Carly died, Scott continued writing every night in their online journal. He shared many of the journal entries in a self-published book called *Carly_Bugg03: A Journey of Faith,* titled after Carly's online nickname.

For months and even years, people across the country responded to Carly's story. Carly's life—and her death—resonated not only with people who had loved her but with complete strangers as well. For a long time, e-mails and letters arrived weekly if not daily. For Scott and Kim, it helped knowing that even though Carly was gone, her influence on others continued.

———

Five years after Carly's death, working late in her office and thinking about the rich and painful journey they had all traveled, Kim wondered if it was finally done, if Carly's life—and her story—had run its course. Carly's angel friends, if they were still around, were invisible once again. Was it time to say good-bye to her daughter and all that her extraordinary life had signified?

Kim gathered her purse and sweater to leave the office. On her way out the door, she stopped by the copy machine to do one last thing. She was still standing there, lost in sad thoughts, when she heard someone calling her name. She looked up.

Someone was waving and hurrying up the hallway toward Kim. It was the young woman who'd thought the balloons and flowers on Kim's desk had signified her birthday.

By the time she got to Kim, she was practically out of breath. She said, "I had to tell you. I got the book about Carly yesterday and read the whole thing last night. It changed my life. I've always believed in God but had walked away from my faith long ago. But not anymore.

I'm going to rededicate my life and my son's life to God. Reading Carly's story inspired me so much. It's such a reminder that there really is something more to life, and to death too."

Brimming with gratitude and joy, Kim couldn't wait to get to her car and call Scott on her cell phone.

"Scott, it's still happening!" she blurted, "Carly's story isn't over after all. . . ."

9

Mountaintop Miracle

—— ✳ ——

Trapped on a remote Arizona mountain, Leroy
and Fran Lane found unexpected help.

Leroy Lane felt uncomfortable, but he kept driving—higher and higher
up a mountain road east of Phoenix, Arizona. Leroy and his family
had recently moved to the Phoenix area so he could recover from
the allergies that plagued him in their native Michigan. Now on this
sunny, ninety-degree Saturday in May 1981, he was taking his family
on an adventure—an exploration of the country surrounding their
new home.

For a self-described flatlander, however, driving a big blue Chevy
van to an elevation past fifteen hundred feet on a narrow, rock-strewn
road was nerve-wracking. Leroy had to concentrate hard on every
switchback as the Chevy climbed. Just twelve inches past the edge

of the asphalt, sometimes on both sides, the road fell away sharply, revealing deep canyons far below. They were so close to the sky Leroy almost felt he could reach out and shake hands with God.

"This is so weird," said thirteen-year-old Mike, looking out the backseat window at the brown, treeless mountain and barren landscape below.

"It's ugly," said his brother, nine-year-old Matt.

Fran, Leroy's supportive wife, didn't comment from her viewpoint in the front passenger seat. But Leroy could tell from the expression on her face that she was equally unimpressed. Their outing was off to a less-than-stellar start.

A moment later, Leroy saw a chance to salvage the situation. Up ahead was a small metal sign pointing left. It read, MORMON FLAT DAM.

Leroy took the turn.

"What are we doing?" Fran asked.

"We're going to see Mormon Flat Dam," Leroy answered. "It's an adventure!"

The adventure included one of the roughest roads Leroy had ever seen. Rocks the size of footballs littered the trail. He slowed to a crawl, but the Chevy still bounced around like a ball in a pinball game.

Finally, the Lanes reached a flat area about fifty feet long and fifteen feet wide that marked the end of the trail. Sheer rock walls bordered the deserted "parking lot" on the right and straight ahead. To the left was a narrow ramp that dropped to another flat area twenty-five feet below. On both sides of the ramp and beyond the lower flat area was a drop-off of hundreds of feet.

The Lanes got out of the van to look around. They discovered another couple that had driven to the lower level in a small station wagon. They also heard the sound of rushing water, but there was no sign of the dam.

"We must have missed a turnoff someplace," Leroy surmised.

"Dad, let's go home," Mike said. "There's nothing here."

Leroy took a last look at their forlorn spot. There was no trail, no marker pointing a way to the dam. He had to admit defeat.

"Okay," he finally said. "Back in the van."

Leroy realized the "parking lot" didn't offer enough room to turn the van around. But he could see the ramp in his rearview mirror. If he could back down the ramp a few feet, it would provide the extra space he needed to maneuver the van and point it toward the direction they had come.

After turning the steering wheel, Leroy inched the Chevy back toward the ramp. He felt the rear wheels descend. But he still needed more room to complete the turn. He backed up some more.

Suddenly, Leroy felt the van's front left side slump.

Uh-oh.

He rolled down his window and peered down.

The Chevy's left front tire was dangling over open space. Leroy cracked the door open to make sure he wasn't seeing things. Sure enough, the view down went on and on. Suddenly, the Lanes were in an extremely precarious position.

"Everybody stay calm," he said—as much to himself as to his family.

He considered the predicament a moment. They were more than fifty miles from home. They were in mostly deserted mountains. His Chevy now blocked the couple in the station wagon below. And since this was long before the advent of cell phones, there was no way to call for help.

No doubt about it—they were in big trouble.

"Okay, everybody get out on the right side," Leroy said in a quiet, firm voice. "Get clear of the van." His family quickly obeyed.

Leroy hadn't been wearing his seatbelt. Now he strapped it on and slowly straightened his wheels. He shifted into drive and attempted to inch forward.

The Chevy had rear-wheel drive, but the back wheels couldn't find traction on the ramp's slippery rock surface. They were stuck.

Leroy climbed out the right passenger door to take a closer look. Fran and the couple with the station wagon joined him.

Leroy shook his head. "How are we going to get this thing out of here?"

"Well, we could push," the other man offered. "We can help you."

"Thanks," Leroy said. "I guess it's worth a try."

Leroy crawled through the right doorway and back into the driver's seat. Fran and the other couple took positions at the back of the van. Leroy put his foot on the gas pedal. But on every attempt, the rear tires simply spun in place. The Chevy didn't move.

"I think you need to give it more gas!" the man called from the ramp.

"Yeah, I think you're right," Leroy answered. "We need more horsepower."

The two boys joined the team at the back of the van. When they were ready, Leroy floored it. He stopped when he heard a *thud*.

Wondering what had happened, Leroy scrambled out the right door again. Everyone was gathered around Fran, who stood there gritting her teeth and examining her leg. Leroy looked, too, and saw a large area on her thigh quickly growing black and blue. When he'd punched the gas, the spinning right rear tire had found just enough traction to grab one of the football-sized stones and hurl it into Fran's leg.

"Fran, I am so sorry," Leroy told her. He felt terrible. He was also more worried than ever. Fran was able to stand but was clearly in pain. Her leg didn't seem broken, but what if her injury was more serious than it appeared? How were they going to get medical attention?

Their adventure was turning into a nightmare.

Leroy didn't know what to do, but he didn't want his family to know that. He got back into the driver's seat as if he had a plan in mind. Then he closed his eyes and bowed his head.

"Lord," he prayed aloud, "I need your help *now!*"

Leroy opened his eyes—and was shocked to see an old Buick LeSabre rattling toward him. It moved within a few feet of the van's front bumper and stopped.

Both front doors flew open, and out stepped two characters that Leroy would have avoided on any other occasion. They were big men, with unshaven faces and dark, scruffy hair that fell to their shoulders. Both wore blue jeans, sleeveless T-shirts, and red bandanas on their heads. They looked like they belonged on Harleys instead of inside a Buick.

"You guys need help," the driver said. It was a statement, not a question.

Leroy wasn't sure if he trusted these men. Their expressions weren't menacing, but they weren't smiling either. Their look was businesslike—they were there to do a job.

No matter their intentions, Leroy couldn't deny the dire circumstances. "We certainly do," he responded.

The Buick's driver positioned himself at the front of the van on Leroy's side while the other man moved to the Chevy's rear.

"Turn your wheel to the right," the driver instructed.

That didn't make sense to Leroy. But even as he doubted, he felt a sense of calm and assurance wash over him. He somehow understood that these men knew what they were doing and would help.

"Okay, back down slowly," the driver said. "Easy now."

Leroy did as he was told.

"Brake!" called the man in back a moment later.

For the next few minutes, the men gave Leroy instructions on how to maneuver the van. They spoke in quiet, confident voices, never contradicting each other. Leroy had the sense they'd done this many times before.

Soon Leroy had all four wheels on the ramp and was backing all the way down to the flat area below. As soon as he was on level ground, he turned his head behind him to make sure his family and the other couple were safe and accounted for.

A second later, Leroy turned his head forward again. He wanted to thank the two men who had appeared out of nowhere and saved him from a frightening scenario.

But the men were gone.

Leroy blinked.

Where did those guys go? he thought. *How did they do that?*

Leroy's mind raced. The two men had been standing close to the van. Even if they'd somehow scampered up the ramp and out of sight in the moment Leroy turned his head, where was the Buick? It would have taken the same maneuvering down the ramp that Leroy had just completed for them to turn around. Even if they had backed out the way they came in—which would have been dangerous and foolhardy—Leroy would have heard them bumping over the rocks through his open window.

Leroy ran up the ramp, his eyes scanning the area for clues, but there were none. The men and the LeSabre had vanished.

Leroy returned to his family. No one had seen the men leave. It was a mystery—but not to Leroy. He'd never seen angels before. Yet there was no other explanation. After all, hadn't they appeared the instant after his prayer?

God sent them, he thought. *He sent helpers at just the right moment to keep the four of us from harm. I have just witnessed heaven's angels coming to the rescue of human beings.*

Leroy's plan for an adventure, which had come so close to disaster, had instead turned into an adventure of faith.

"Thank you, Lord," he said aloud. "Thank you. Thank you. Thank you."

Leroy has talked about what happened at Mormon Flat Dam many times since. "Some people, after I tell the story, still doubt the presence of actual angels. You can see their expressions turn skeptical, and I can almost see their minds coming up with rational explanations," he reflected. "But I don't care! Those men—or rather, those angels—gave me such a strong feeling of the presence of God that I will never doubt. I will always remember and give thanks to Him."

PART THREE

Mischief-Makers

The devil's minions seek to harass, confuse,
and distract people from the truth.

"My dear Wormwood . . ."

If you recognize that salutation, chances are you've read *The Screwtape Letters*, the classic epistolary novel by C. S. Lewis. First begun as a series of short pieces for a magazine, then gathered into book form in 1942, this little volume tackles big issues about demons and, moreover, the way human beings think, act, and are led astray.

The story is a collection of letters from a senior demon, Screwtape, to his nephew, a junior tempter named Wormwood. The mentor schools his apprentice in the ways to deceive, delude, and discourage his assigned human, a British man known only as "The Patient." Those of us who deplore bureaucracy, administrative minutia, and the endless red tape of modern life will be amused to find that Lewis, even in the 1940s, portrays hell as a hierarchy (actually called a

"Lowerarchy") with rules, procedures, a devilish corporate ladder to climb, and even a House of Correction for Incompetent Tempters. Throughout, Lewis sprinkles in thought-provoking gems about human nature, including:

- "The safest road to hell is the gradual one—the gentle slope, soft underfoot, without sudden turnings, without milestones, without signposts."[1]
- "The humans live in time but our Enemy [God] destines them to eternity."[2]
- "All mortals tend to turn into the thing they are pretending to be."[3]

In the end, it is revealed that the Patient has been killed during a World War II air raid and has been transferred from earth to heaven. Wormwood is punished for letting a soul "slip through [his] fingers."[4]

Since one of Lewis's most popular books featured demons (which he referred to as devils), what was his counsel to people in dealing with these dark and devious entities? In short, acknowledge their presence and afford them due respect, but don't confer too much power on them. He said:

> There are two equal and opposite errors into which our race can fall about the devils. One is to disbelieve in their existence. The other is to believe, and to feel an excessive and unhealthy interest in them. They themselves are equally pleased by both errors and hail a materialist or a magician with the same delight.[5]

In the pages that follow, we describe several encounters with demons—in contrast to Lewis's fictional account, the ones we present really happened. The intent is not to perpetuate Hollywood-style sensationalism, but to portray how Satan's minions seek to mislead and misinform people. A few foundational thoughts should be kept in mind:

If you believe the Bible is true, you ought to believe that demons are real. Nearly everyone believes in angels—probably because they are bright, helpful, and full of goodness. Many people don't believe in demons—probably because they are dark, harmful, and full of badness. Nevertheless, the Bible contains so many references to demons, demon possession, unclean spirits, exorcisms, healing, and the casting out of evil spirits that we must allow for the reality that the universe is more complex and mysterious than it may appear to our senses. If Jesus encountered demons and evil spirits during his lifetime on earth, his followers likewise may face them.

Demons have less power than Satan, who has far less power than God. Again, Lewis's insights are helpful: "I believe in angels, and I believe that some of these, by the abuse of their free will, have become enemies to God and, as a corollary, to us. . . . They do not differ in nature from good angels, but their nature is depraved. *Devil* is the opposite of *angel* only as Bad Man is the opposite of Good Man. Satan, the leader or dictator of devils, is the opposite not of God, but of Michael [the archangel]."[6] Why is this important? Because Christians—children of the Living God—can rely on God's power and provision. God is the Creator of all things, including demons, and he holds all authority.

Harassment of humans falls on a continuum—and possession is rare. Most people these days form their perception of demons from hyped-up Hollywood fare. They walk away from films such as *The Exorcist, The Exorcism of Emily Rose,* and even cheesy horror flicks like *Night of the Demons,* thinking demons take possession of people all the time and cause them to behave like feral animals. Such wild, demonically induced behavior does happen—but rarely.

There is a huge difference between demon affliction (being bothered, harassed, troubled) and demon possession (being inhabited).

Affliction can be explained as a spectrum that ranges from demonic influence *on* a person to the extreme of a demon actually *in* a person's body. One way to understand this concept is to consider the way alcohol makes a person drunk. We know that the first sips cause changes and reactions, gradually going from relatively mild to more pronounced. As more and more is consumed, the body's responses become more noticeable (bloodshot eyes, slurred speech, loss of coordination). It is a progression of *levels* of inebriation: sober . . . tipsy . . . drunk.

This analogy describes the continuum from demons *on* to a demon *in* a person. This continuum is demonstrated as a gradual progression of influence—from low-grade affliction to eventual possession (complete bodily possession generally is rare, despite what we see on the big screen).

Demonic possession and various stages of demonization have been documented for thousands of years in cultures worldwide. The anthropologists, psychologists, sociologists, ministers and priests, and dedicated laypersons who have devoted their lives to studying such supernatural activity report an amazing consistency in the encountered cases.

Are demons real? We believe they are—just as real as angels. But those who believe in God and recognize his power need not tremble at the thought of a demon appearing. Yes, they are malevolent mischief-makers, not to be trifled with or toyed with. And, yes, they have spiritual abilities greater than humans . . . but much weaker than our ultimate protector and provider, God.[7]

10

Dueling in the Dark

For Ross Purdy, an out-of-the-blue phone call
led to an intense spiritual battle.

Sitting in his book-lined church study on a Friday afternoon in late
February 2000, Ross Purdy was prepping Sunday's sermon when his
secretary put a call through, saying it sounded urgent.

When he picked up the phone, the voice on the other end said
almost breathlessly: "I've got a problem. But I need to tell you first,
pastor, that I'm not crazy. My name is Kent, and I'm a sheriff's deputy.
I'm not some kook."

"I understand," Ross assured the man. "I'll be happy to help if
I can."

"What do you think about ghosts?" Kent blurted. "Really, I'm not crazy. But I want to hear what you know about ghosts and spirits. Do you believe in poltergeists?"

Ross, pastor of Lake Arrowhead Community Presbyterian Church in Lake Arrowhead, California, was respected in the picturesque small town nestled in the mountains above San Bernardino Valley. The friendly, gracious thirty-five-year-old talked with community members regularly and sometimes took out-of-the-blue calls—but this one was surely more out-of-the-blue than most.

His first thought was, *Why didn't you call the Roman Catholic Church or a denomination that emphasizes supernatural activity more? Why not talk to a priest or pastor better versed in the spirit world?* Nevertheless, he launched into an explanation about angels and demons and how they fit into the spiritual hierarchy described in the Bible.

Ross realized he was dispensing far more theological background than Kent probably wanted. He stopped and asked, "Tell me, what's going on? What's the real reason for the call?"

Kent exhaled loudly. "I've never believed in this stuff before, but my wife and I don't know what to do. We've got strange things going on in our house. Unexplainable things. The kinds of things you see in movies."

Asked to elaborate, Kent told of objects moving without being touched. Plates scooted across the kitchen counter while he and his wife, Dana, cooked. Utensils fell to the floor even though no one stood within ten feet.

Then he mentioned his three-year-old son, Dylan, who regularly played in the basement. Recently he had been speaking to someone, or something, he called Frankenstein. The boy's parents initially chalked it up to his active imagination, just playtime fun and games. But when other inexplicable phenomena began occurring, they wondered if everything might be connected.

He ended by saying again, "I'm a sheriff's deputy, and I don't know if all this is real or not. But when our son talks about seeing a man walking around in the basement, it's definitely time to do something."

Ross could hear the desperation in the man's voice. "I'll certainly try to help—and soon—but let me ask you one thing: Why did you call *me*?"

"Yours was the first name I came across in the phone book," he answered. "We don't go to church and don't know any ministers. So I'm grateful for your help."

Checking his calendar, Ross suggested he go to their house the following afternoon. He asked that they find a place to take their son so he wouldn't be frightened. And he said he'd like to bring along another pastor.

"Good thinking," Kent said. "It's always smart to bring backup."

The next day at one o'clock, Ross met a fellow pastor named Dale who led the Community Bible Church in town. A tall man with an ample midsection, Dale had relocated to the area from Austin, Texas, and people in the lakeside town were drawn to his gentle drawl, quick laugh, and corny, cowpoke humor. In the four years he'd been at Lake Arrowhead, he had become a respected and recognizable leader.

The two men hopped into Dale's Ford pickup and rumbled down Rim of the World Highway along the lake. It was a cold and gray day with low-hanging clouds hovering overhead. As they drove, the pastors discussed their approach to the meeting ahead: Their main purpose, they agreed, was to share biblical truths for whatever the situation turned out to be. They concurred that the family needed to have a foundation of faith and belief in Jesus Christ.

A few minutes later, Ross said, "Dale, I seem to recall your mentioning you've had experiences with the occult and spiritual warfare, right?"

"Yep, I sure have—more than a couple," he answered. "You never know what'll happen, but we'll hope and pray for the best."

"That reminds me," Ross said, pointing to a pullout on the road, "let's stop and pray before we get to the house."

Crunching over remnants of the last snowfall on the ground, Dale maneuvered his pickup to stop a safe distance from passing cars. Over the sound of the heater warming them against the chill outside, both men took turns praying. Ross prayed that if they were about to encounter malicious spirits, their hearts would be pure and any evil would be revealed. Dale focused on seeking God's protection from any harm.

After they said their *amens*, Dale declared, "All right, then, I think we're covered. Let's go."

Ten minutes later, Ross and Dale strode up to the door of the house—a neighborhood home built on a hillside with a lodge motif. Kent and Dana welcomed the pastors, mentioning that a neighbor was watching their son. As Dana hung up their jackets on a coatrack, she told them how grateful she was that two clergymen were there to help "stop all this weirdness."

Kent, with his muscular build and clean-cut appearance, looked very much like a sheriff's deputy, as he had been so determined to let Ross know he was. He and his petite brown-haired wife exchanged glances, and he said to Dale, "I know it sounds crazy, but really, we're just normal people."

"We believe you. You've got some concerns about things going on here," Dale said, his faint lilt taking the edge off a tense situation. "We're going to see if we can bring peace back to your home."

Ross mentioned that anything shared or revealed during their time would be held in strict confidence. Then they all sat down in the living room, the couple taking seats on the couch, and the two pastors opposite them in cushioned chairs. Ross and Dale shared what the Bible has to say about the spiritual world and gave an overview of Christian belief. Ross mentioned that he didn't believe in ghosts per se, but certainly believed in evil spirits. And while evil spirits are real, God is the ultimate authority over everything. His Son Jesus is the power, and his very name makes demons tremble. After nearly an hour of discussion, Kent and Dana said they would like to become Christians, and the two pastors led them in a simple prayer of salvation.

Then the couple took Dale and Ross on a tour of the house. They all moved into the kitchen, and Kent pointed to the counter where dishes had slid several feet on their own. He pointed to a clock that had seemed to jump off the wall. He told of hearing objects fall to the ground in rooms that were unoccupied.

They proceeded to Dylan's bedroom, where he had spoken to shadows in the corner. Dana explained that at times he seemed to be engaging in discussions with them and answering questions.

Next the couple showed the two pastors a stairway that led to a large basement, which was used as a family room and their son's play area. Kent and Dana decided they would wait upstairs.

As the two guests descended the stairs, Ross felt a sudden chill in the air—an extremely cold space. But he told himself not to get too worked up about a drafty spot in the house. The two began walking and praying, and after several minutes Dale stepped into a laundry room around the corner from the stairs. Ross wandered around, noticing a small, dark alcove apparently used for storage.

Soon Ross went to rejoin his colleague. As he turned the corner, he was stunned.

Dale had stepped out of the laundry room and was crouched down with his back against the wall. He was huddled in an almost fetal position, and his face wore an expression of pain and fear.

Ross hurried toward him. "Dale, what happened? Are you okay?"

He stayed near the floor, silent. Finally he said in a near whisper, "I'm okay. Just give me a few minutes. I'll be all right."

Ross couldn't help but notice how visibly shaken Dale appeared. "I'm going to keep praying—for this house and also for you."

As he paced around the room, Ross felt a strong impression that he should pray while walking up the stairway. Halfway up the stairs, still praying for Dale and against any evil in the house, he suddenly felt himself thrown back against the wall. *Wham!* It was as if an invisible wrestler had body-slammed him.

Up against the wall, he felt a large pair of hands choking his throat.

He continued praying—more frantically and now silently since he could not speak or breathe for the next several seconds.

Heavenly Father, help me. I rebuke this evil in the name of Jesus Christ!

Immediately, the pressure ceased from around his neck, and he gulped in air.

Then, adrenaline coursing through his body, he sensed something moving, something he couldn't see. Though he couldn't visibly detect it, he had no doubt something was there. He followed the being or entity as it entered the dark storage area. It was as if this evil thing had retreated to its shadowy hole for safety. Still praying, Ross asked Jesus to remove all evil.

He descended the stairs and walked around the corner again, finding Dale on his feet but breathing hard and perspiring. "Are you okay?"

"Yes," he replied. "I think I was being spiritually oppressed. I'm okay now."

After another ten minutes in the basement, they walked back upstairs and said a prayer for Kent and Dana. Ross told them what had happened and that they had prayed over the entire house.

"I think our prayers have taken care of the situation," Ross said. "Besides, you are now followers of Jesus, and he doesn't share his holy presence with darkness." Ross assured them he would follow up soon.

Dale said very little in parting. His usual jovial demeanor had vanished.

As soon as they left, Ross again asked Dale what had happened.

"I felt spiritually attacked." He didn't seem to want to say more.

Arriving back at the church parking lot, Ross suggested they pray together before going their separate ways—since obviously something powerful had just transpired. They uttered a short prayer and left, saying few words as they went.

The following Monday, as Ross sat in his church office, a phone call came from a friend in the community.

"Did you hear what happened to Pastor Dale?"

Ross immediately felt a gnawing irritation that his partner in Saturday's ordeal had told someone about what occurred—against their confidentiality agreement.

But the person on the phone continued. "I can't believe it. It's just come out that Dale has been having an affair. Apparently it's been going on for months and involves a teacher at the high school. It's so sad. I hate to tell you—I just thought you needed to know."

Ross would later learn that a parishioner at Dale's church had begun to suspect immoral behavior and felt God's urging to confront him. When she did—the day after the encounter with an evil spirit—the pastor dropped to his knees and confessed everything.

But at the moment, Ross sat at his desk in stunned silence, thoughts and feelings swirling and churning.

How awful for Dale and his family.

That sure explains a lot about Saturday's events.

What a dangerous position to put himself—and me—in.

That demonic encounter may not be over after all.

Later that night, while he was still at church, Ross's wife, Kathy, called and asked him to come home immediately. She sounded panicky. It turns out that as Kathy and their five-year-old daughter, Katy, sat on the living room couch, they both heard a deep growl as if an animal were behind them. Katy screamed and held tightly to her mom. Kathy looked over her shoulder; nothing was there. But then she felt a hand hit the back of her head and watched as Katy's hair was ruffled from behind.

When Ross arrived, he found them in a different part of the house, holding on to each another. They all prayed together and no other incidents occurred.

———

Two days later, Ross called four friends from other churches whom he knew to be people of integrity and prayer. He scheduled an appointment to return to Kent and Dana's house for follow-up prayer. The couple told him nothing had changed since the pastors' visit a few days earlier—the strange occurrences had continued. Ross thought he knew the reason why.

With Dylan again staying with neighbors, the five guests, along with Kent and Dana, walked around the house and prayed. They decided to keep their prayer simple, asking Jesus to make this his home and to drive out all darkness. The group moved steadily through the house, feeling unified and confident.

But the drama wasn't over yet. Ross felt a strong urging to stay in the boy's bedroom to pray after the group left for the next room. He felt led to open the closet door and pray inside it. When he opened the door, he saw two little boys sitting inside clinging to each other, trembling, with fear on their faces. Then, fading away slowly, they disappeared.

Ross called for the others. Without mentioning what he had just witnessed, he asked Dana what she knew about the house's previous owners.

"All I know," she said, "is that two boys used to live in this house with their father. He was a drug addict and used to abuse them. We heard that they used to hide all over the house from their dad."

There's no way this could all be a coincidence, Ross thought. He revealed what he'd seen and the group prayed some more.

After two hours of prayer at the house, the team left, all reporting a deep sense of peace and serenity. Ross kept in touch with Kent and Dana, and they did not have another incident of anything "weird." They went on to join a church in the area and to grow in their new-found faith.

And what became of Pastor Dale? He revealed his affair to the congregation a week after he was confronted, and he resigned from pastoral ministry. He and his wife moved to another part of California, worked through the painful ordeal, and stayed together. Some time later, Dale took an administrative position for a Christian ministry.

Reflecting on his experience, Ross says: "It certainly made the reality of Scripture come alive in a vivid and powerful way. The New Testament tells us, 'For our struggle is not against flesh and blood, but against the rulers, against the authorities, against the powers of this dark world and against the spiritual forces of evil in the heavenly realms.'[1] Ministry, as with faith in general, is about living the kingdom, not just talking about it. If we preach Christ, we will find opposition, especially spiritual opposition. But the great news is that Jesus has power over all things."

One more thing, he adds: "Angels are real, and so are fallen angels—evil spirits. If you're going to tangle with dark forces, you had better be filled with the light."

11

Evil Comes Home
to Roost

———— ✳ ————

When Dorothy Hedin encountered a demon,
she found a unique solution to
removing the menace.

It had been an especially long and tiring day. Summer was always a busy time around the Hedin place—a two-story country home that lay at the edge of the dense Pacific Northwest rainforest near Eugene, Oregon. Dorothy lived there with her husband, Rusty, and two teenage sons, Carl and Garth.

Late one evening in the summer of 1978, the day's chores were finally done, and the sun had set at last. Some days it seemed the work would never end. Dorothy and Rusty, an insurance agent by day, kept a variety of farm animals on the property surrounding the house—chickens, rabbits, sheep, geese, turkeys, and a couple of pigs. On top of the routine care and feeding of the animals, Dorothy fought a running battle with wild predators from the nearby forest that were determined to take their share of the family's livestock. That night, Dorothy finished cleaning up in the kitchen, turned out the lights, and headed gratefully toward her bedroom for what she hoped would be a good night's sleep.

But peaceful slumber was *not* what lay ahead.

To reach the door to her ground-floor bedroom, Dorothy had to pass by the bottom of the sweeping circular staircase that ascended to the second floor. The house was quiet and the light in the hallway was dim. Seventeen-year-old Carl was in his room at the top of the stairs, doing homework or getting ready for bed himself.

"Carl was a good young man, trying to live a Christian life," Dorothy said of her younger son. She worried at the time that his Christian values might be making things hard on him at school, but he never gave her reason to fear he was in danger of losing his faith or getting into serious trouble. He was a source of comfort and joy to her.

As she walked toward her room that night, Dorothy happened to glance up the staircase. What she saw sent a chill through her body and stopped her in her tracks.

"The best way I can describe what I saw is to call it a 'heat wave,'" she said. "It looked like the shimmering air you see rising off hot pavement at a distance in the summertime."

The disturbance in the air was limited in size—as wide as the staircase, but only three or four feet high—and was advancing slowly but steadily up the stairs toward the door to Carl's room. It made no sound and gave off no heat or odors. Instead, it emanated a different kind of energy—a blast of menacing hatred that Dorothy recognized immediately.

"I felt an intense wave of evil coming from the thing on the stairway," she said. "It felt very dangerous. All of a sudden, I just *knew* it was a demon and that it was headed toward Carl to do him harm. I can't explain how I knew; I just did, without stopping to think about it."

Dorothy was not the sort of person who is obsessed with evil spirits or prone to seeing demons around every corner. In fact, she gave them no thought at all, having never encountered one before. The Nazarene church she attended placed more emphasis on serving a loving God than on fearing Satan and his minions. Even so, she was no stranger to the idea of spiritual warfare.

"During those years, I did feel like the devil was after my family," she confided. "We'd had some really hard times. The devil never let us alone. It seemed like there was always something negative going on."

Her sole thought as she stood looking up at the demonic presence advancing toward her son's room, however, was desperation and determination that she had to do *something* to protect him. She instinctively understood that if she didn't, the demon would "enter Carl's body." She sensed the evil spirit was strong and very determined to reach its goal.

Dorothy instantly began to plead with Jesus to protect Carl and to force the demon back down the stairs away from her son. It was an anguished prayer of such intensity that it immediately drained her physically and emotionally. She cannot say how long she stood there fervently begging God to intervene—a few minutes at most—but the "heat wave" stopped ascending the stairs and started back down.

"Even when the demon began moving down toward me, I never felt afraid for myself, only for Carl," Dorothy recalled.

Although God appeared to have answered her prayers by forcing the demon to turn away from Carl, Dorothy felt it was not enough. She remembered something her pastor had once said on the subject of spiritual warfare. It was his belief that when casting out a demon, one should ask God to send it into another living creature—just as Jesus did when he freed two men from a multitude of demons by sending them into a herd of pigs.[1]

Intent on preventing the demon's return, Dorothy raced to think of a way she could follow that advice. What came instantly to her mind was the image of a young rooster in her chicken yard named Le Le. He was a red-and-black bantam with a long plume of shiny dark tail feathers.

"We had other animals, but Le Le was all I could think of," Dorothy said. "I begged God to send the demon, which was still moving toward me, into that rooster."

All at once the evil, shimmering heat wave disappeared. Dorothy didn't see it leave the house or enter the rooster, but she had no doubt it was gone. She collapsed onto the stairs in exhaustion and gave thanks to God for hearing her prayer. She felt confident that he had done exactly as she asked and had sent the demon into Le Le.

"I felt so tired, like I had worked hard since sunup," she said. "But it wasn't the kind of tired where you can go right to sleep. I can't put into words how shaken up I was. It stayed with me for hours. But the Lord assured me that it would be okay, that he had taken care of matters. I was so relieved that Carl was safe."

The next day, Dorothy confided the details of her harrowing experience to her pastor's wife, Faye, in spite of her fear of ridicule. To her relief, Faye shared stories of her own experiences with spiritual warfare, confirming Dorothy's conviction that the incident was real, and that her response—to call on God for help—was the only correct one.

In more than thirty years since then, Dorothy has never again been called upon to do battle with a demon. Though she still wondered many times if she had imagined the whole thing, God always gently reassured her that it really did happen.

Dorothy still lives in her forest home in Oregon with her husband, Rusty. Eventually, her family got through the hard times they'd suffered back then. Today, Carl is a successful Christian businessman and the father of two kids of his own.

As for Le Le, he was never the same.

"I know roosters can be really mean without having a demon in them," Dorothy joked. "But after that night I couldn't go anywhere near the chicken yard without him jumping on me."

Though Le Le had never threatened anyone in the family before, he began to attack Dorothy every time she came near, flapping his wings menacingly and pecking and clawing her with his sharp spurs.

"More than once he made me bleed," she said. "A few times he even jumped up on the back of my neck when I bent down for the eggs. It was scary, but I always figured it was a small price to pay for keeping Carl safe."

Ever since the night of Dorothy's prayer, the rooster seemed intent on vengeance. Indeed, Le Le's barnyard battle with Dorothy persisted until he died of old age several years later.

What advice does Dorothy have for those who might one day find themselves in her shoes?

"Demons are real—believe that," she said. "I've experienced it firsthand. But all you have to do is pray. Call out to God and believe that you will be protected. And you will be."

12

Fight for Freedom

— ✳ —

Glen and Linda Vance were determined not to
give up on the young woman
tormented by demons.

For nine months, Glen and Linda Vance did everything they knew to do, but the demons refused to leave Shahla alone.

Shahla had come to America from Iran several years earlier to attend college in Oklahoma. When one of her professors, Dr. Forest Ladd, told her about Jesus Christ, Shahla liked what she heard about this loving and powerful God—so different from the god of Shahla's Muslim upbringing—and she converted to Christianity.

While attending a local church, Shahla met Glen and Linda Vance and eventually agreed to be mentored by Linda. It seemed like Shahla's search for a new life in America had led her to new spiritual life as well. Yet Shahla seemed conflicted. Even though she truly wanted to learn more about this loving God, she often stood Linda up when they tried to meet for coffee and Bible study. She also struggled in her relationships with God and with people. And when she fell in love with a young man from Jordan and got married, Shahla experienced depression and anxiety and was unable to consummate their relationship.

Glen and Linda noticed something else disturbing. Shahla seemed to have a strange relationship with the spirit world. One evening she mentioned a conversation she'd been having with a friend of hers who lived in another state. Linda said, "Really? You two have been talking on the phone?" To which Shahla shrugged and said, "We don't need the phone. I talk to her in my mind."

Shahla also believed she had the ability to heal. When Glen and Linda's daughter Robin complained of a headache, Shahla offered to cure the girl by commanding the headache to leave Robin and go into a lamp across the room.

That evening, Glen gave Shahla a copy of the book *The Beautiful Side of Evil* by Johanna Michaelsen, about malicious spirits that can influence us and seduce us into bondage. As Shahla read the book, she recognized herself in its pages time and time again. She asked Glen and Linda for help.

One night the couple visited Shahla and her husband, Nick, at their apartment. After an enjoyable evening, Glen and Linda were preparing to leave when Glen said, "I'd like us to pray for Shahla before we go."

As Glen prayed, he suddenly heard a deep masculine voice begin to curse him. Glen's eyes flew open and he looked around the room. The voice came from Shahla.

It was already ten o'clock at night, but the Vances knew they needed to help Shahla find freedom from the spirits tormenting her. They prayed with Shahla for four grueling hours, commanding the spirits to leave. The spirits would weep and, always in masculine voices, beg to be left alone. Four times, Shahla began to gag and cough, eventually spitting something up. Each time this happened, she seemed more relaxed and at peace.

Around two in the morning, Glen and Linda left the couple, convinced that at least four spirits had been dislodged. Perhaps there were more, but that was a start.

The next morning Nick phoned to say that after the Vances left, Shahla had driven straight to the home of a spiritualist friend who "restored" everything the Vances had undone, inviting the evil spirits to reclaim their place in Shahla.

Over the next six months, this happened many times. Each time, Shahla would cry and insist she wanted to be free, but that she didn't know if she could live without the spirits. "These are my friends," she would say through tears. "They've been with me as long as I can remember. I don't know if I can live without them."

Glen and Linda were followers of Jesus and had been involved in church and ministry for years. In fact, they were in the process of launching an urban ministry called The Salt Mine so they could serve disadvantaged people throughout their city. Indeed, praying for people and helping them walk in greater freedom was something Glen and Linda had been doing for a long time.

But this . . . this felt out of their league. Convinced they needed help, the Vances called various churches and ministries, looking for anyone who had more experience. And yet even when they found seasoned veterans who agreed to pray for Shahla, nothing seemed to change for their young friend.

Sometimes the Vances were told by well-meaning people that Shahla needed to accept Jesus as her Savior and then the problem would be solved. And yet Shahla *had* believed in Jesus Christ back when she was in college. She *was* a Christian, and yet the dark spirits tormenting her seemed entrenched.

One night a young pastor named Jim from a local denominational church joined the Vances to pray for Shahla. When Jim showed up with a list of references for good psychiatrists in the area, Glen suspected that Shahla's problem would prove out of Jim's league as well.

Sure enough, as they prayed for Shahla, the young pastor became visibly shaken. Every time he mentioned the name *Jesus,* Shahla laughed maniacally at him in a deep masculine voice. At one point, Shahla herself became frightened and, looking around, cried out, "The whole room is filled with smoke and I can't see any of you!"

Later, Jim said to Glen and Linda, "I've got to have time to digest this. None of this is fitting into the grid they gave me in theology school!"

———

In the following days and weeks, Jim began to reread his New Testament, looking for answers. When Jim had decided to follow Jesus a number of years earlier, he'd been immersed in the drug culture. After becoming a Christian, the changes in his life had been radical, even miraculous. Yet while attending Bible college, Jim was led into a more rational way of thinking. He graduated convinced that God doesn't do miracles anymore, that spiritual warfare with demons was a thing of the past, and that experiences with the supernatural were to be frowned upon.

Suddenly his experiences with Shahla were telling him something different. He continued searching the Bible, and the three of them continued to meet with Shahla and pray for her deliverance.

One day Jim said to Glen, "I told my bishop about Shahla and the things I'm learning that the Bible says about spiritual warfare."

"And?" Glen asked.

Jim said simply, "He fired me."

Yet it was a turn of events Jim couldn't regret, not when he knew he was discovering the truth.

And still the battle to free Shahla raged on.

On dozens of occasions evil spirits were cast out of Shahla. And each time, she sought the help of a spiritualist to restore what had been displaced. Eventually Shahla's husband, frustrated that she was unwilling to consummate their marriage, gave up, filed for divorce, and returned to Jordan.

Late one Friday night as the Vances slept, Linda sat up in bed and shook her husband's shoulder. "Glen, wake up, honey. I keep seeing pictures in my mind."

Awake now, Glen listened carefully as his wife told him about the vision she was having. Finally he said, "Let's pray. If these pictures are from God, let's ask him to make them even clearer to you."

As they prayed, Linda saw the pictures again. There were seven of them and as she described what she was seeing, Glen wrote everything down.

The first image was simple. Linda saw someone with an injured, oozing eye.

After that, Linda saw a series of images, each involving a child or young girl, and each more horrifying than the last. The first image was of a child sitting on an old man's lap on a crowded train. Another was of a little girl being stuffed in a dresser drawer by a man. The child kept crying and screaming and trying to get out, but the man would not relent.

Glen and Linda had no idea what any of it meant. All they knew for sure was that if God was preparing them for something, he would make everything clear in good time.

The next morning Glen left to meet some volunteers helping him renovate an old building he had rented for The Salt Mine ministry.

Around noon, he got an urgent call from Linda.

"Glen, come home quick. Shahla's here. And you're not going to believe this, but her left eye is swollen shut and oozing."

Glen raced home. Sure enough, Shahla looked exactly as described on the phone. Glen and Linda asked God to heal Shahla's eye. By the time they said "Amen," Shahla's eye was completely healed and back to normal.

Glen got the list he had written the night before, detailing the images Linda had seen. The first image of the injured, oozing eye had just come true. Linda asked Shahla about the child on the train.

Shahla began to cry. She told Glen and Linda that when she was a little girl in Iran, she and her mother often rode crowded trains to get from one place to another. Since seats were limited and often given to the elderly and disabled, Shahla's mother usually ended up standing, balancing Shahla on her hip as they were pressed and jostled in the horde of passengers. One day Shahla's mother asked an old man if her daughter could sit on his lap during a long train ride. He agreed and ended up quietly molesting Shahla while her mother stood nearby in the swaying crowd.

Linda asked Shahla about the remaining images one by one. Each represented an event in her childhood during which she had been sexually molested, sometimes violently.

Shahla wept. She seemed to regress as well, becoming more child-like as the Vances described the images from Linda's vision.

Glen and Linda began to pray over each image, speaking in authority to the demon that had used a little girl's terror at that moment as an entry point into her life. Each time they commanded a demon to leave, Shahla would cough and the demon would be gone. A few of them were more difficult to get rid of, causing Shahla to gag and even vomit.

The sixth demon was the most powerful. It didn't leave as readily as the others had. Instead, it defied Glen and Linda in the same low masculine voice they had heard before.

"I don't want to leave," it growled through Shahla. "You have no right to tell me to leave. You have no authority here."

Glen spoke right back. "No! *You* are the one with no authority here. Jesus Christ is Lord of Shahla's life. She belongs to him, not to you. She doesn't want you anymore. We command you to go."

The demon spat curses and obscenities. Glen responded with truth and Scripture. Over and over again.

Suddenly it released her. Shahla gagged and spit and coughed—then collapsed, limp like a rag doll on the floor. Glen and Linda immediately asked God's Spirit to fill Shahla completely with his peace and presence.

That night Shahla had a dream.

She dreamed she was in a vast underground cavern, but walking up a staircase leading to heaven. Looking down, into the cavern below, she could see the many people who had abused her, including a witch who had put a curse on her. All of them were reaching for Shahla, trying to grab her and pull her back into the darkness. Yet Shahla didn't flinch or hesitate. She continued walking confidently up the stairs, into the sunlight of the open sky above, until she was free at last.

That was more than twenty years ago. Since then, Shahla married and had two children, a son she named Forest Ladd after the professor who introduced her to Jesus, and a daughter she named Sumer.

Jim, the pastor who had assisted, and his wife, Teri, started a thriving church called Dayspring Christian Fellowship in Woodland Park, Colorado. More than ever before, Jim knows that people really can be healed and restored in their spirits, bodies, emotions, and relationships through Jesus Christ. He says these days he not only prays *for* the impossible, but serves the God who can *do* the impossible.

As for Glen and Linda, the urban ministry they started more than two decades ago is still impacting lives in their city, and not a week goes by that they don't find themselves praying for someone seeking freedom from spiritual bondage.

"Linda and I understand so much more today about spiritual

warfare than we did when we were fighting so hard for Shahla," Glen said. "That was our first experience with the dark side. It was our boot camp, so to speak. But God is good, and his love for Shahla—and for each of us—is greater than whatever chains would leave us bound and shackled."

Even after all this time, whenever Shahla talks about her relationship with Jesus—and about the darkness from which she was rescued—she does so with passion and fire. "You cannot touch my faith," she said. "Christ is everything to me. When you are possessed, you are powerless. That was my experience. I was powerless and under the control of dark spirits. And then a greater power came in and freed me, and that power is Jesus Christ."

She adds: "Demons are real. Many people don't think they are real, while other people know they are real and live in fear. But after all I went through, I can honestly say I'm not afraid, but confident. And it's not because of me, but because of him. It's because I have a heavenly Daddy who will take care of everything, and I don't have to be afraid anymore."

13

Kitchen Table Conflict

— ✳ —

Pastor Ross Purdy unexpectedly confronted
two determined spirits.

Ross Purdy smiled, stood at the doors exiting the sanctuary, and
waited. The lead pastor of Burbank Presbyterian Church in Burbank,
California, he'd already delivered his sermon and was now prepared
to greet people leaving the service. His work for the day was nearly
done, and he was ready to go home and enjoy some family time on
this warm Sunday in the summer of 2009.

While the parishioners filed out of the sanctuary, a handful of
people lingered to ask questions about the sermon or to offer thanks
for the message. Ross was finishing one such conversation when he
noticed a fortyish woman with shoulder-length blond hair and brown
eyes making her way toward him.

Uh oh, he thought. *I bet I know what this is about.*

In a moment, the woman was beside him. Julia was the single mother of two daughters. She smiled, but behind the pleasant expression was a look of concern.

Ross could guess why. Though he hadn't been there, he'd been told about the church-sponsored youth retreat the weekend before. Julia's fifteen-year-old daughter, Marissa, had smuggled in an Ouija board. She'd apparently used it to try to contact spirits of the dead and had encouraged other girls on the retreat to try it too. The retreat leaders eventually found out and took the board away.

Ross wondered if Julia was unhappy about the way the church staff had handled the situation.

"Hi, Ross," Julia said. "I'm wondering if we could talk. It's about my daughter."

Ross thought this might require more than a quick and casual conversation. "Sure," he said. "The best thing is to send me an e-mail, and we can set up an appointment for later this week. How's that sound?"

A strange look—was it fear?—flashed across Julia's face. But she quickly recovered her composure. "All right," she said. "I'll do that."

Ross forgot about the conversation until later that afternoon, when he mentioned it to his wife, Kathy.

"You know, Ross, I think you should call her," Kathy said. "She spoke to me this morning when she picked up her kids after Sunday school. She sounded really concerned, almost panicked."

Ross made the call and was surprised at Julia's story. Marissa, it seemed, had moved past the Ouija board. Now she was calling on spirits directly. What had seemed like innocent teenage game-playing had taken a much darker turn.

The night before, Marissa had been awakened in her bedroom by the feeling of something clutching her ankle. She looked up and in the shadows saw a man standing there, a smile on his face, his hand wrapped around her leg.

Marissa repeatedly tried to jerk away, but the man wouldn't let go. When Marissa tried to crawl off the bed, the man yanked her back. He never stopped smiling.

Marissa screamed.

The sound woke up Julia. She raced down the hall and threw open her daughter's bedroom door. She saw Marissa writhing in bed, but there was no sign of the man. The intruder had vanished.

Ross wasn't sure what to make of the story. Most likely, he figured, it was the case of a teenager with an active imagination. Or too many hormones, too many scary movies, excessively graphic video games—who knows? But he also believed in the reality of the spirit world, both good and evil. After all, he'd had encounters with dark forces in the past (see the earlier story "Dueling in the Dark"). He told Julia that he and Kathy would come over that evening.

The night was getting dark but staying warm when Ross and Kathy arrived at the front door of Julia's home. The one-story house was actually a converted garage with a small living room and kitchen. Marissa slept in the single bedroom, while Julia and her younger daughter converted the front room into a shared bedroom each night.

Ross thought of himself as a typical guy in most ways, not nearly as intuitive about his environment as his wife. But when he walked through Julia's front door, something got his attention.

Whoa, something's not right, he thought. *There's darkness here. This feels wrong.*

Kathy took Julia's younger daughter outside to play while Ross, Julia, and Marissa went on a quick tour of the house. Marissa had long, dark hair, a round face, and large, expressive brown eyes. She told Ross about other strange things that had happened, especially in the bathroom, where objects that had been on the counter mysteriously ended up on the floor.

While they were in the bathroom doorway, Julia interrupted with her own story. "I'm not crazy," she said. "I was in here a few days ago and a ceramic angel that used to hang on the wall, right there, suddenly flew across the room and smashed against the other wall. It was like someone had thrown it at me."

Ross could sense the fear in both of their voices. *What's going on here?* he wondered. *Is this just their imaginations, or Marissa wanting attention, or is it something more?*

The three of them sat down at the kitchen table, where Marissa explained further about her recent attempts to converse with the dead. She'd been speaking with two "spirits," a boy named Daniel and an adult named Isaac. She believed that Isaac was the man in her bedroom the night before. She wanted Ross to make Isaac go away, but she wanted Daniel to stay because he was a "good spirit."

Ross asked Marissa how she spent her time when she was alone. She said she was fascinated by the idea of demonic possession. She watched shows about it on TV and researched it on the Internet. She'd been freaked out by the movie *The Exorcism of Emily Rose.*

Ross thought, *No wonder she's frightened and panicked.*

"You know, Marissa, you really shouldn't be messing around in that world," Ross said. "It's not good for your mind. The Bible actually forbids talking to spirits this way. You're opening your life up to things that are forbidden by God."

Marissa seemed to think about this for a moment. In a quiet voice, she asked, "Am I in danger?"

Ross took a breath. "Let me ask you something first: Have you given your life to Jesus Christ?"

Marissa shook her head.

"Then you need to make a decision. I think you need to accept

Jesus as your Lord and Savior. With him you have nothing to fear. Without him you have everything to fear."

Ross leaned forward, resting his elbows on the table, and locked in on Marissa's big eyes. "Marissa, would you like to invite Jesus Christ into your life?"

Ross couldn't believe what happened next. The moment he finished his question, the chair beneath him—a typical wooden kitchen chair, from which he'd just taken his weight off—slid back with an audible scrape.

He turned quickly. No one was there.

The chair had moved more than two feet.

Oh boy, he thought. *I did not do anything to move that chair. Someone does not want to let her go.*

Ross turned back to face Marissa and Julia. Their eyes were open wide.

"Okay," he said. "You both saw what just happened, right?"

The women nodded.

"I'm not going to let that distract me from what I was just asking you," Ross said. "Marissa, would you like to invite Jesus Christ into your life?"

"Yes," she said. "Yes, I would."

"Then I think we should pray," Ross said. He bowed his head. "Marissa, we're all sinners, saved by the grace of God and the blood of Jesus Christ. Will you now invite him into your life?"

"Yes," Marissa said. "Jesus, I want you to come into my life."

Ross knew Marissa didn't understand everything that had just happened. They continued to talk. Marissa asked, "Can I still talk to spirits? I'd still like to talk to Daniel."

Ross shook his head. "I think you need to make a choice here," he said. "These spirits are generally from the Evil One. Remember, someone was just in your bedroom pulling on your ankle. Jesus comes to bring peace, not fear. If you're communicating with spirits that bring fear, I can promise you they're not of God. So let's pray about that now too."

Again, Ross lowered his head and began a prayer. "Lord," he said, "I ask that you would protect Marissa, Julia, and this household from any spirits that are not of you. I ask that any other spirits would leave right now."

Marissa suddenly interrupted: "Did you hear that?"

"I didn't hear anything," Ross said.

"Neither did I," Julia agreed.

"I just heard this shriek right next to me," Marissa said. "Then it got fainter, like it was moving away."

When Ross and his wife left the house, he encountered a very different feeling than when he'd arrived. He felt peace and calm.

A few days later, Ross returned to the house with a team from his church. They again prayed the home and family. Neither Marissa nor Julia has been visited by spirits since.

Ross isn't ready to embark on a new career as an exorcist. But the experience has been a reminder to him that the spirit world is real. It calls to mind the words from the apostle John: "Every spirit that does not acknowledge Jesus is not from God. This is the spirit of the antichrist, which you have heard is coming and even now is already in the world. You, dear children, are from God and have overcome them, because the one who is in you is greater than the one who is in the world."[1]

Ross added, "It's easy to go to church, hear the sermon and the teaching, and forget that things haven't changed since those words were written two thousand years ago. We're still in a fight with darkness—but we still have the power to overcome. It's the power of God."

PART FOUR

Fond Farewells

A window between this life and the next opens routinely—
in the eyes of the dying.

The Hall of Hewn Stones was packed with angry men that day. Their voices reverberated off the walls in a loud rumble of righteous indignation, all aimed at one man who stood alone before them. He had been dragged off the street to face charges of blasphemy against the Law of Moses. Death hovered above him, because a verdict of guilty—a likely outcome—would be swiftly followed by execution.

Built into the north wall of the temple in Jerusalem, half inside the sanctuary and half outside, the hall was the meeting place of the Sanhedrin, the "supreme court" of ancient Israel. The Romans ruled the streets outside, but within these walls seventy-one religious judges retained full authority over the hearts and minds of the people.

The accused, a man named Stephen, was a follower of Jesus, the troublemaker these men thought they'd seen the last of after they arranged his crucifixion at the hands of the Romans. But no! Apparently, his infectious message lived stubbornly on.

"All who were sitting in the Sanhedrin looked intently at Stephen, and they saw that his face was like the face of an angel."[1] Perhaps this new rebel now stood in precisely the same spot as his Master before him. But where Jesus had remained mostly silent as he faced his accusers, Stephen had plenty to say. He pulled no punches as he gave this learned assembly a history lesson in the long line of God's prophets who were persecuted and murdered by their ancestors for speaking the truth. In summary, Stephen condemned those present for killing the very Messiah about whom the prophets spoke.

That was the last straw. The hall erupted in noise and fury. Stephen had just sealed his fate, and his death was imminent.

> But Stephen, full of the Holy Spirit, looked up to heaven and saw the glory of God, and Jesus standing at the right hand of God. "Look," he said, "I see heaven open and the Son of Man standing at the right hand of God."
>
> At this they covered their ears and, yelling at the top of their voices, they all rushed at him, dragged him out of the city and began to stone him.[2]

You may read this story and think that moment-of-death visions like Stephen's are the rare privilege of exceptionally holy saints and mystics. That's an understandable conclusion. You might also think that such glimpses of glory only occurred in the early church times—the period when the book of Acts was written, when miracles of all sorts seemed to be as numerous as the new disciples joining the Christian church. Based on the stories we have heard, including those we are about to relay, we would like to challenge those assumptions.

As the stories in this section reveal, deathbed glimpses of what awaits us are remarkably commonplace. People who approach death slowly, and with awareness, often report that the ordinarily impenetrable barriers between worlds become see-through and porous well before our final crossing. They see angels in the room or deceased loved ones waiting for them on the other side. They hear music or voices telling them there is no need to be afraid. They see bright and beautiful scenes displayed before them.

We personally believe that the benefit of these visions can be summed up in one word: *comfort*. For the living and for the dying. For those about to cross over, the experience offers reassurance that death is not the end of existence, but only a doorway to another realm—perhaps even one populated with angelic beings and familiar faces.

Some doubt whether we'll recognize each other when we get to heaven. But in Scripture David speaks of a future reunion with his son who had died.[3] There is biblical support for heavenly rendezvous with our loved ones.

Indeed, many of these experiences are a source of encouragement years after the fact and are passed down like family heirlooms. For instance, there's the story of Tunzel Gilliland, who lost her first husband and first child in a flu epidemic in Texas during the early 1900s. Throughout her life, she recalled the heartrending sorrow of looking out her bedroom window and watching family members bury her deceased infant in the field by the farmhouse where she lived. She hadn't even been allowed to hold her baby.

In 1978, decades after the loss of her child, Tunzel approached death at Bethany Hospital in Bethany, Oklahoma. Her granddaughter Lin sat by her bedside when the elderly woman suddenly looked up toward heaven, raised her hands, and exclaimed, "There's my baby! There's my baby! Oh, I'm finally going to get to hold my baby." Shortly thereafter, she passed from this life into the next—no doubt to be reunited with the child she had lost so many years before.

Another encouraging account features Coral Butcher, who steadily moved toward death through a battle with cancer. She stayed in the parsonage of Skyline Wesleyan Church in San Diego to be cared for by her son, Orval, the founding pastor of the church, and other family members. As it became apparent that her time on earth was drawing to a close, Coral's husband, children, and grandchildren gathered around her bed. Since she had always loved music, Orval sat at the piano in the room and everyone began singing "My Home, Sweet Home." As they all sang the last verse from Coral's favorite hymn—"Life's day is short—I soon shall go, to be with Him who loved me so"—she abruptly sat up, looked upward, and smiled brightly. Her granddaughter Sharon remembers how she called out the names of family members who had gone before. As she breathed her last, her family continued singing: "My beautiful, beautiful home. Home, sweet home. . . . I see the light of that city so bright—my home, sweet home." Years later, this sacred scene bolsters the faith of Coral's descendants and friends.

Deathbed visions like these are a great source of consolation for those who are left behind. Grief after a loss is often dominated by the need to know that our loved ones are not simply "gone," but continue to live on in another plane. Having heard from their own lips what the dying have seen on the other side—and that it is *good*—goes a long way toward helping us let them go and get on with living our own lives. Furthermore, we gain confidence that our present separation is only temporary. One day it will be our turn to be welcomed by those who've gone before us.

William Winter wrote, "As much of heaven is visible as we have eyes to see." The stories that follow are an invitation to gather at heaven's window and have a look for yourself.

14

Welcome Home

On his deathbed, Charles Kimbrough saw his
beloved wife and knew he would be reunited
with the love of his life.

"I sure love those kids of yours, Shari. They've brought so much joy
to my life. Remember that time we juggled milk containers in Shelbi's
school cafeteria? And when Patrick and I marched down the street
playing those trumpets I bought, pretending to be a parade band?
What a hoot!"

Charles Kimbrough chuckled as he said the words, clearly relish-
ing the memories. His two grown children, Shari and Denise, stood
by his bedside in the dark Oklahoma City hospital room and laughed
too. But there was sorrow behind the laughter and smiles. Their father
was dying.

It had been a difficult five years for the close-knit Kimbrough family. In 2000, Judie Kimbrough—Charles' wife and Shari and Denise's mother—was diagnosed with multiple myeloma. Judie struggled and suffered with the cancer for a year before succumbing in March 2001 at age sixty-two.

For Judie's daughters, grandchildren, and especially Charles, it had been a devastating loss. Charles and Judie met when they were in eighth grade, wed when he was nineteen and she was eighteen, and shared forty-three years of married life together. Partners in every sense of the word, they enjoyed a rare and radiant love, as if the innocent and passionate blush of teenage romance had never faded. Charles, handsome and athletic, pursued a professional baseball career before earning a bachelor's degree in science education and a master's degree in microbiology. He taught for years in high schools and junior colleges, and then became an assistant school district superintendent.

In her work life, Judie was secretary to a pastor and a counselor. But her most important role was as Charles' strength behind the scenes. She supported and encouraged him through all the joys and trials that come with being a father, educator, and community leader.

A compassionate and godly woman, Judie also encouraged her husband in his faith. Charles believed in God, but the scientist in him wanted empirical evidence to rely on. They often talked about it at the kitchen table after church.

"Judie, how can you just believe?" he'd ask.

Patting his hand, Judie would answer, "Charles, I don't know. It's all in God's Word and I believe it. It's as simple as that."

"Well, honey, I need to *see* a miracle," he'd respond. "If I saw a miracle, I'd believe without any question too."

For Charles, his wife's excruciating illness and death was not only an emotional blow, but a spiritual one as well. After a visit with Judie at the hospital, he talked about it with Shari while sitting in their car in the parking lot.

"How can a loving God let a precious woman like your mother

go through something like this?" he asked, tears of anger and frustration stinging his eyes.

Shari tried to find the right words. "Dad, I understand what you're feeling, because I feel it too," she said through her own tears. "But here's the thing: Suppose she's right about God and the Bible and heaven. Why take the chance of not being with her again? That's the bottom line."

Despite words of reassurance to their father, Shari and Denise also struggled after their mother's death. Shari felt angry and bitter toward God. Her trust in him wavered. At a low point, she thought, *I could do just as well without this.* Denise's faith was stronger, yet she also felt empty and sank into a depression that plagued her for years.

It was Valentine's Day 2005 when the Kimbrough family learned from doctors that Charles, age sixty-six, had pancreatic cancer. Shari and Denise, who were just beginning to heal from their mother's death, were stunned. The shock wave to their family, and their faith, was doubly devastating.

How could the God I've heard about since I was little allow something like this to happen? Shari thought. One cherished parent ripped away prematurely because of cancer and then the other likely to follow? It was all too much. Where was this loving, compassionate God?

Charles, on the other hand, discovered an unexpected strength. It was as if he realized that the time for questions was past. He finally knew in his heart what he believed. Though he was deeply concerned about leaving his daughters and two grandchildren behind, he did not fear death.

"I've got to tell you girls something," he said to his daughters. "I certainly don't want to go through cancer and all the treatments after seeing what it did to your mother. But think of it this way: The worst possible outcome would mean that I'll get to go and be with your mom—and in that case, the worst thing would be the best thing. If I die, I'll get to be with the person who was my partner, lover, and best friend nearly all my life."

For several months, treatments kept the cancer at bay. Charles continued to work and play golf as before. But on December 9, he entered the hospital to examine a buildup of fluid in his belly. The cancer, they all learned, had metastasized to his abdomen.

Shari and Denise rearranged their schedules so they could be with their father around the clock at the hospital. Charles' health declined quickly, and he drifted in and out of sleep.

It was during the wee hours of Wednesday night and Thursday morning, December 14 and 15, that Charles and his daughters reminisced about better times. Shari stood at one side of the bed and Denise at the other. It was agonizing for them to watch their dad, once a proud and strapping athlete, wither away. The unspoken anger toward the Lord still gnawed at their souls.

When awake and alert, Charles continued to reflect. He told Shari and Denise how proud he was of them and how much he loved being their father. He talked about how blessed they all were to be in a family so close and connected.

Suddenly, in the middle of a conversation, Charles's eyes shifted from his daughters toward the ceiling.

"What's that smoke?" he asked.

Denise's eyes darted back and forth. "What smoke, Dad?"

"Up there," he responded. "And why did that tile move?"

Shari and Denise, following their father's gaze, stared at the ceiling. Nothing had changed.

"It's not moving, Dad," Shari said.

"Yes, it is," he declared. "Right there."

The daughters exchanged glances, their eyebrows raised.

"Well, I don't know, Dad," Denise finally replied. "Maybe they're doing some work on the hospital." She didn't know what else to say.

Charles continued to stare intently at the ceiling. Suddenly he gasped.

"*Judie,*" he whispered.

Shari and Denise looked again at the ceiling. They still saw nothing unusual. Yet Charles, his eyes wide, his mouth smiling, remained fixed on the vision only he could see.

"I've missed you so much," he said in a gentle voice. Then he raised his arms and wrapped them around himself, as if giving someone a tight and loving embrace.

"You're so beautiful," Charles whispered again. "It's so good to see you."

Shari and Denise stood in shocked stillness. What was happening here?

In the middle of his conversation, Charles turned to Shari. "How's my breath?" he asked. "How's my breath?" Shari was too stunned to reply.

The dialogue—one-way from Shari and Denise's perspective—continued for a couple more minutes.

"Judie, it's just so good to see you," Charles repeated.

Then he glanced away from the ceiling, the meeting apparently over.

After a moment, Charles, beaming and bright-eyed, reached out a large hand to each of his daughters.

"Girls," he said, "I want you to tell everyone you know that it's there. It's really there."

Shari knew exactly what he was referring to—heaven. She found her voice. "Dad, we will," she replied.

"You've got to," Charles said. "You've got to tell everyone. There's no doubt it's there."

Charles then closed his eyes and fell asleep.

Shari and Denise were amazed. Their father was a practical man, never prone to theatrics. He was on very little pain medication. To claim that he'd just glimpsed his wife in heaven was completely out of character.

They could conclude only one thing: The encounter was real.

As the rest of Thursday unfolded, Shari and Denise continued to be amazed. Word of Charles's dire condition had gotten out. Friends, colleagues, and former students streamed into his room to pay a final visit to the man who had touched their lives in so many ways over the years. Yet rather than acting like he was on his deathbed, Charles seemed energized.

"Hey, how are you doing?" he greeted each person who walked in the door. "Guess who I saw yesterday?"

"Who's that?" the guest would ask.

"Judie and Jesus," Charles answered.

Usually, the person would look over at Shari or Denise.

"Yes, he did," they said with a smile.

That night, after all the visitors had gone, Charles stopped communicating and slipped into semi-consciousness. By early evening of the next day, he labored to breathe. Shari and Denise, along with a cousin and friend, were at his side. Soon they were joined by their pastor.

After a few words of Scripture and comfort, the pastor said, "Girls, let's see if we can sing him into heaven." They chose the hymn "Amazing Grace."

Their gentle voices filled the room: "Amazing grace, how sweet the sound . . ." Charles's breathing relaxed. By the start of the second stanza, he was no longer in his earthly body.

Shari and Denise clung to each other and sobbed. It was another heartrending loss. Yet they also felt great peace. They knew without a doubt that Charles had joined his wife and his Savior in heaven.

"Being there when he saw Mom and reached out for her, I have no doubt it really happened," Denise said. "It's an extra boost for my belief and faith."

Shari added, "It was such a comfort and gift to us. I miss them both tremendously, but I have the assurance that we'll see them again. My anger at the Lord and my mistrust—that's all gone. I have no questions now about heaven, and I never will."

Both daughters agree that a grand reunion took place the day Charles joined Judie in heaven . . . and another homecoming is yet to happen when it's their turn to be embraced by open, eager arms.

15

The Final Ascent

— ✳ —

After a rock-climbing accident, Bobby Mason passed on—but not before sharing a glimpse of heaven with his best friend.

Bobby Mason died on a beautiful spring day in May 2008. He left this world as he might have chosen to, if he'd had time to give it any thought—outside in the open air, with the sun on his face and the earth at his back.

Forty-one-year-old Bobby spent the last morning of his life—indeed, the last few moments—in the company of his best friend, Alex, doing what they loved more than anything: rock climbing. Bobby died slowly, and with no apparent pain, at the base of his favorite route on the vertical wall of the Black Canyon in western Colorado.

But his death was far from a silent slide into oblivion. In fact, normally a man of few words, Bobby had plenty to say about what he saw in the moments before he departed for good.

It had been an unusually cold and snowy winter. Bobby lived in a small corn-farming town called Delta, where the Gunnison River emerged from the steep and narrow Black Canyon, just a few miles from its confluence with the Colorado River. He worked at an auto parts store most of the year, saving enough money to spend his summers on the rocks. While some in the sport sought after product endorsements as a way to pay the bills, Bobby preferred to stay clear of the distractions that came with corporate money—and to just climb.

The day he died was the first opportunity of the year to make his favorite ascent. It had become a tradition for him to start the season on this particular route. For one thing, the hardest part of the whole climb—the crux—occurred within the first one hundred feet, a challenge that appealed to Bobby's sense of adventure. After a rather routine beginning up to about thirty feet, the route's difficulty level rose dramatically.

"We had done this climb together many times," said Alex, a science teacher at the local high school and two years younger than his friend. "It was almost a ritual with us. That day we flipped a coin to see who would climb and who would be on belay. Bobby won the toss."

For all but the most adventurous, climbing is a two-person sport. The person on belay remains on the ground to take up the slack in the climber's rope with a special belaying device clipped to a harness. Should the climber fall, the person on belay must respond instantly, using the device to apply enough friction to the rope to keep his or her partner from falling very far—usually only as far as the previously placed anchor in the rock. To be on belay is to have another person's life—literally—in your hands. Over the years, Bobby and Alex had learned to trust each other completely, and they rarely climbed with anyone else.

That day Bobby was especially excited as Alex double-checked his rigging. He'd been away from the rocks longer than usual, waiting for the last of the snow and ice to melt. Sure, he could travel to other locations where conditions improved sooner, but he preferred to start the year off right.

"I'd never seen him so eager to get going," Alex remembered. "I joked with him about having a date at the top, but I knew that for him reaching the top wasn't the point. He enjoyed every reach and every hold along the way."

Finally harnessed and ready, Bobby took a deep breath and placed his hands on the base of the wall.

"On belay?" he asked Alex.

"Belay on," came the expected reply.

Climbers—safe ones, at least—take nothing for granted and communicate thoroughly before making a move.

"Climbing."

"Climb on," said Alex. He was ready to assume his duty.

Bobby let out a whoop and began his ascent. He was a traditional climber, not a sport climber. That meant he always placed his own anchors in the rock rather than relying on equipment left behind by others. He preferred it that way for safety reasons—he trusted himself to do it right—but also because it gave him a greater sense of conquest and accomplishment, knowing he might have been the very first person in history to do the climb in precisely that way. Instead of pitons, which must be hammered into the rock, Bobby's tool of choice was an invention called a cam. Once inserted into a wider gap in the rock face, it is designed to expand outward and hold tight when the force of a climber's weight is applied.

That day, Bobby rose quickly through the first section and reached the crux of the climb in no time. He placed another cam into the rock before proceeding.

"Here we go," he called out to Alex below, who tested his own footing on the ground, alert and ready. Alex knew the next fifty feet of rock face was smooth and relatively featureless. It took great skill and strength to find and exploit the tiny fissures and ledges that were present. Sometimes a climber chose well and found an invisible pathway forward, one miniscule hold leading to another. Sometimes every choice seemed to lead to a dead end.

"At first Bobby was tearing it up," Alex said. "Everything was going right. Then he came to a standstill and decided to backtrack a step or two. That's when it happened."

When Bobby changed direction, his right foot slipped from the half-inch lip of rock where he'd placed it. It was enough to unbalance him.

"Falling!" he called out, alerting Alex to be ready to catch him.

Bobby let go of the rock, expecting to drop only a few feet before being stopped by the rope threaded through the last cam he'd placed. Such falls happen all the time and typically pose little danger. They are jarring, perhaps, but nothing more. Usually the worst part is knowing that you are giving back territory you'd already climbed.

Not this time. Alex quickly and skillfully took up slack in the rope as Bobby fell, but when the rope went taut against the anchor, the metal cams broke free from the wall as they expanded. The winter ice had weakened the rock enough that it gave way under Bobby's weight. It was a climber's worst nightmare.

Alex moved backward as fast as he could over the loose rock at the bottom where he stood, trying to take up the sudden slack, but it was too late. There was nothing he could do to stop Bobby from falling all the way to the ground.

"I watched him drop like it was happening in slow motion," Alex said later. "I wanted to believe he'd be okay, but part of me knew better."

Alex ran to the spot where Bobby lay. Miraculously, he'd barely missed a large and jagged boulder. Instead he landed on a flat, muddy patch of earth just a few feet wide. Still, the impact was enough to cause severe injury. Bobby lay on his back, conscious, but unable to move.

"I was terrified," Alex recalled. "We were miles away from anyone or anything, and I knew I'd have to leave him there to go for help. I told him that and was blubbering on about how sorry I was that I'd let him fall. But he smiled at me. There didn't seem to be any pain in his expression, just this warm, peaceful smile."

"Don't go," Bobby said. "It'll be all right."

Alex was about to argue, but the look on Bobby's face stopped him. His friend looked upward past him. His eyes went wide with wonder.

"Oh man, you've got to see this," he said. "Unbelievable."

"What is it?" Alex asked, captivated by the air of calm that had come over his friend.

"A beautiful green field," Bobby said haltingly. He was having difficulty breathing but didn't seem to notice or care. "I've never seen flowers like that. So many. So *bright.* The light is in the flowers and grass, like that's what they are made of. And music. Unreal! Can you hear that?"

Alex thought he almost *could* hear it, seeing the powerful effect it had on his friend. Bobby's face lit up and tears filled his eyes–tears of joy.

"They're all there!" Bobby said. "Waiting for me!"

"Who?"

"My grandma and grandpa. Uncle Daniel! He looks so good."

Alex knew Bobby's grandparents had died when he was a boy. His uncle Daniel passed away only the previous year, after a long battle with cancer. He was barely more than a skeleton by the time the disease had taken him.

Bobby strained to get the next words out, but he spoke of seeing friends he'd known welcoming him and urging him forward. He talked more of brightness, vivid colors, and how people looked so happy.

Alex sat quietly beside his friend, knowing the end was near.

"Okay," Bobby said. "They say it's time to go, brother. I need to go. Don't worry. Please don't worry. I'm okay."

Bobby died six minutes after his fall, but for Alex time had stood still. For those few moments, eternity seemed to wrap its arms around them both. He felt as if he'd been to heaven and back himself, in spite of his overwhelming pain at losing his best friend. Alex cried all the way into town. And all the way he heard Bobby's voice in his mind repeating again and again: "Don't worry. I'm okay. It's so incredibly beautiful."

And Alex believed it.

16

A Time for Letting Go

------ ✳ ------

Could Pam Burton's determination keep her
severely injured son from crossing into
the next life?

"Mom!"

Through the phone line, Pam could hear the panic in her youngest son's voice.

"Someone called and said Kevin was in a crash on a bridge!" Chris
blurted. "They're transferring him by helicopter from Winnsboro to
the hospital in Tyler right now!"

Pam had been running errands in Tyler, Texas, all morning. At
that moment, she happened to be fifteen minutes from the hospital
where her eighteen-year-old son, Kevin, was being flown, instead of
at her home in Alba almost an hour away.

She drove as fast as she could. As she pulled into the parking lot, a helicopter was hovering noisily above the landing pad in front of the hospital.

A glass blockade kept Pam from rushing onto the helicopter pad. From a distance, she watched as paramedics slid open the doors and pulled out an emergency gurney laden with a shrouded figure. Pam ran alongside the glass, staying parallel with the paramedics as they wheeled the gurney toward the hospital entrance. Near the entrance, the blockade ended, and Pam ran to her son.

Kevin was unconscious and bleeding from his nose and ears, his head and face swollen and still swelling. Shocked, Pam fell back as the paramedics pushed Kevin through the emergency doors and disappeared.

Frantic, Pam began to pray.

Lord, if Kevin dies, I'll kill myself! I couldn't take it. I couldn't go on without him. You've got to let him live, please God . . .

Forty minutes later, Pam was still standing outside pleading with God when several cars pulled into the parking lot. In moments, she was surrounded by half a dozen family members, including her ex-husband, Charles, and sixteen-year-old Chris, the son who had called Pam nearly an hour earlier with the news. A few minutes later, Kevin's fiancée, Gae, arrived with her mother.

Charles wrapped his arms around Pam. They were both crying.

"I got to the hospital in Winnsboro just as they were putting him on the helicopter," Charles said.

"Charles . . . what happened?"

The words tumbled from his mouth. "He was in a speedboat on the lake with three friends. Going under a bridge, the boat hit a concrete piling, and Kevin was thrown from the boat into the piling."

Pam closed her eyes. "I can't believe this is happening. Will he be all right?"

A doctor came outside and approached the family. After a brief introduction, he said, "I have bad news. Kevin has massive brain damage. He's not going to make it through the night. I'm sorry."

Suddenly, his voice sounded farther and farther away. Pam remembers crying. She remembers sliding to the ground. And then everything went black.

Pam awoke on a bed in a small room where the nursing staff had placed her until she could regain consciousness. Her mom and sister were with her and, when she felt strong enough, the three women joined a growing number of family and friends in the waiting room. Charles was describing Kevin's condition to several newcomers.

"Kevin's on life support right now, but it doesn't look good," he was saying with a pained voice. "The doctor says he's never seen anyone with that much brain damage make it."

Gae's eyes were still red from crying. A pretty girl with auburn hair, she was a year older than Kevin and had just started college to become a veterinarian. She enjoyed everything her fiancée enjoyed—animals and hunting and fishing—although she hadn't tried bull roping yet, which Kevin was learning to do and loved.

As everyone continued talking and processing the news, Gae began to hyperventilate, then shake. Someone called for a nurse as Gae went into a full-blown seizure brought on by shock. Several nurses helped her into a wheelchair and took her to a private room for sedatives and observation.

All through the night, Pam prayed like she'd never prayed before, always pleading for Kevin's life. "Take me instead," she begged. "He's too young to die. I can't live with this, Lord. I'll take my own life if anything happens to him. I can't bear the thought of going on without him."

The next morning, Kevin remained in a coma. But he was still alive.

Over the next several days, Pam refused to leave and refused to sleep. Her greatest fear was that if she left the hospital for even a few minutes, Kevin would die while she was gone. So she stayed. And prayed.

One afternoon Pam asked Kevin's doctor, "Is there any hope? You said he wouldn't make it through the night, but he's made it this far. Can you give me a percentage of his chances?"

The doctor shook his head. "I don't like percentages."

"I'm not asking you to put it in concrete," Pam persisted. "Just give me a percentage."

"All right, Pam," the doctor said with a frown. "Maybe 10 percent."

Pam breathed a sigh of relief. "OK. Thank you. At least that's something. At least you're not saying there's no chance."

The doctor looked pained. "Look, Pam, Kevin is still on life support because he still has some brain activity, but not much. I don't know why he's still alive. That's why I'm saying 10 percent. It's not because I've seen anyone with his injuries ever survive. It's just because Kevin's still hanging on, and none of us can figure out why."

Every few hours, the ICU nurses allowed three visitors at a time to sit with Kevin. Visiting times were brief, about thirty minutes. Knowing how much Gae and Kevin loved each other, Pam often let Gae stay with Kevin the full half hour while other family members rotated in and out.

One night during visitation, Chris and Pam found themselves alone at Kevin's side. Chris turned to his mom and said, "Do you think he's going to make it?"

"I hope so, Chris. He's lived this long . . . maybe he'll make it."

Chris and Kevin had always been close. Now the sixteen-year-old just nodded, wanting desperately to have hope.

"Chris," Pam admitted softly, "ever since the accident, I keep hearing Kevin's voice. Over and over. He keeps telling me to let him go, that everything will be okay and I need to let him go. But I can't do it."

Chris looked up, alarmed. "We can't let him go, Mom."

"No, we can't," Pam agreed solemnly. "And we won't."

Five days after the accident, Kevin's doctor met with the family. "Kevin is fading. He won't last till morning, and there are some decisions we need to talk about."

When he asked Pam and Charles about organ donation, Pam exploded.

"You're not going to touch him!" she yelled. "We're not donating any organs! He's going to be fine!"

After the doctor left, Charles and other family members began planning Kevin's funeral, talking about who would officiate at the service, who would serve as pallbearers, and what music Kevin would want.

As she had many times since the accident, Pam heard Kevin's voice. Once again, she heard him clearly say, "Mom, let me go. It's going to be okay." Once again, the answer formed in her thoughts. *I can't let you go, Kevin. I can't.*

The next morning, Kevin was still alive.

Mid-morning, one of Pam's girlfriends arrived at the hospital. "Pam," Janice said. "I feel like the Lord wants me to pray for Kevin."

Pam got permission to take Janice with her into the ICU to see Kevin. As Janice prayed for healing and peace, a feeling of calm came over Pam. After a few minutes, Janice excused herself and left the room.

Pam stayed with Kevin through the afternoon. She studied her son. He had jet-black hair, just like hers. His striking green eyes were swollen shut, and Pam wondered if she'd ever look into those beautiful eyes again.

Walking to the window and staring into the now dusky sky, she suddenly felt her son's presence very strongly in the room. She felt that he was awake and present in spirit even though he remained in a deep coma. At the same time, she felt a second presence, one she felt certain was Jesus. Then she heard someone speak, as clearly as if that person were standing next to her in the room.

"Pam," the voice said, "I want you to go to the hotel across the street and get a good night's sleep. Tomorrow morning at ten o'clock, I'm going to take Kevin home with me."

Greater peace than she had ever known flooded over Pam. When she returned to the waiting room, several family members saw the calm on her face and jumped to their feet.

"What happened?" someone asked. "Did he come out of the coma?"

"No," she said, "everything's the same."

Except that it wasn't. At least not for Pam. For the first time in six days, she had peace.

She left the hospital and checked into the hotel across the street. Accompanied by one of her sisters, Pam slept soundly all night long. She awoke the next morning and, still peaceful, walked back to the hospital, where the rest of the family were still keeping vigil.

"The doctor said they were taking him for another MRI," Charles told her. Pam just nodded.

At ten o'clock, the doctor appeared and asked Pam and Charles to come with him into the hall where he told them simply, "I'm sorry. He's gone."

Pam didn't cry. Instead, she said, "Thank you. I know you did everything you could."

Back in the waiting room, Chris told his mom, "I know you didn't want to talk to the doctor about donating organs, but Kevin signed the permission form on the back of his driver's license. It's what he wanted."

Pam looked at Chris, then at Charles. "Really?"

They nodded.

"If that's what Kevin wanted," she said, "then that's what we'll do."

Kevin's heart was donated to a man who later wrote to Pam, letting her know that, as a result of Kevin's decision, he had been given more time with his grandchildren. Two women had their lives extended after each received one of Kevin's kidneys.

Several months after Kevin died, Charles and Pam were together in Kevin's room, sorting through books and photos, hats and boots and roping gear.

Pam sat on Kevin's blue-striped bedspread, holding his pillow to her face. "It still smells like him," she said.

Charles stood near the bedroom doorway. "I knew Kevin was going to die."

Pam nodded. Charles had eventually told her that when he saw Kevin in Winnsboro shortly after the accident, a doctor told him the injuries were so severe that recovery was all but impossible. Charles had known from that moment that there was very little hope. From the day of the accident, he'd understood what Pam had been unable to grasp until God gave her a supernatural peace, six days later.

Now Charles looked at Pam, still holding Kevin's pillow. He said, "But even though I knew he was going to die, I also knew everything was going to be okay."

"How did you know?" she asked.

"The whole time we were there, I kept hearing Kevin's voice. He kept saying 'Let go, Dad, just let me go.'"

Pam stared at Charles. With awe in her voice, she said, "He kept telling me the same thing."

Charles said through tears, "He knew. He knew he couldn't be saved. His spirit was there and wanted to leave, but he couldn't. Not until he knew we would be okay."

Following Kevin's death, Pam went on to create a ministry home for troubled girls. More than a thousand girls have come through the ministry, which Pam calls Holy Highway. Some stay for a year, others for just a few months. They attend school, get counseling, and find a fresh start away from the drugs or other influences that have wreaked havoc in their lives. Pam says that helping other parents and kids who, for whatever reason, can't be together for a while has helped her find a measure of healing.

Pam keeps Kevin's picture on her desk in her office at Holy Highway. Kevin would be a man by now with children of his own, but there are never any new photos to update the old. To Pam, her son is still eighteen and always will be, and the girls often ask about the handsome dark-haired boy with the beautiful green eyes.

PART FIVE

Many Happy Returns

If a deceased loved one pays you a visit, should you . . .
Rub your eyes? Run? Or rejoice?

The beloved author and minister Frederick Buechner recounts a dream involving a friend who had recently died—a "very undreamlike dream." The deceased friend stood in his room, and Buechner said, "How nice to see you. I've missed you."

"Yes, I know," the man responded.

"Are you really here?" Buechner asked.

The friend replied, "You bet I'm really here."

Seeking tangible reassurance, Buechner asked, "Can you prove it?"

"Of course I can prove it." And the friend threw Buechner a piece of blue string, which he caught.

"It was so real that I woke up," he recalled.

The next morning over breakfast, Buechner reported the incident to his wife and the friend's widow, who happened to be visiting.

When he mentioned the blue string, his wife called out, "I saw it on the rug this morning!"

Buechner hurried to the place his wife had seen the bit of blue string and, sure enough, there it was. "I knew it wasn't there last night," he said.

He concludes: "Either that's nothing—coincidence—or else it's a little glimpse of the fact that maybe when we talk about the resurrection of the body, there's something to it."[1]

When you hear a story like this—or more dramatic cases of deceased loved ones appearing and even interacting with those still living—you likely have one of three responses:

You don't believe it. "Sure, lots of strange things happen," you protest, "but seeing dead people and that kind of thing is all in the imagination—or just an odd coincidence of circumstances. Great stuff for scary movies, but not for real life."

You're skeptical but open-minded. "Some of those stories sound pretty far-fetched," you might say, "but anything's possible, especially with the mysterious world of the afterlife."

You are convinced these experiences do indeed occur. "Why doubt phenomena we can't fully understand from our time-bound, earthly perspective?" you might be asking. "Since we live in a spiritual world among spiritual beings, we shouldn't be surprised when supernatural events happen."

Should you find yourself among the dubious and doubtful, it's possible that you fear the interference and influence of psychics, mediums, clairvoyants, and the like. You've heard too many spurious stories, seen too many 1-800-PSYCHIC ads on TV, and perhaps even known people duped by charlatan palm readers. That is a legitimate and justified concern.

Let us say clearly and emphatically: Seeking out communication with the dead is a boundary that must not be crossed. Under no circumstance should someone *solicit* communication with or *summon up* the presence of the deceased. Why? Doing so would expose ourselves to deception on the part of unscrupulous purveyors or, worse, open our lives to the darkness of evil spirits. Most of all, God gave explicit instructions on the matter: "Let no one be found among you who . . . practices divination or sorcery, interprets omens, engages in witchcraft, or casts spells, or who is a medium or spiritist or who consults the dead."[2] And again, "Someone may say to you, 'Let's ask the mediums and those who consult the spirits of the dead. With their whisperings and mutterings, they will tell us what to do.' But shouldn't people ask God for guidance? Should the living seek guidance from the dead? Look to God's instructions and teachings! People who contradict his word are completely in the dark."[3]

Having said that, let us point out that there is a vast difference between *asking for* a dead person's appearance and *acknowledging* it when it comes without solicitation. What we are talking about here are when deceased family members or friends appear to you unbidden and unrequested—when they come looking for you, not vice versa.

We should mention our personal views on this topic, which we agree upon. When we wrote our previous book, *Heaven and the Afterlife,* we were in the second category mentioned above: open to the possibility that such visitations happen but fairly skeptical and suspicious. Our opinions began to change during the writing of that book, as we came across plenty of research that revealed this phenomenon is quite common. One study found that 64 percent of bereaved people who responded had an afterlife encounter of some kind following the death of someone close, and 98 percent of those said the experience had given them great comfort.[4]

But we became thoroughly convinced when we started researching the book in your hands. That's because we talked with or corresponded with scores of people who reported the appearance of a dearly departed loved one. Frankly, we were shocked at how many of these accounts came to us. And these people we heard from are not wacky, out-on-a-limb types—they are credible and reliable men and women, many of whom we know personally. These are professors, pastors, business owners, attorneys, military personnel, and the like—folks typically regarded as sensible and down to earth.

For those who remain dubious, you might consider that there is precedent for after-death visits found in the Bible. For instance:

The appearance of Moses and Elijah. One time Jesus took his disciples Peter, James, and John up on a high mountain. "There [Jesus] was transfigured before them. His face shone like the sun, and his clothes became as white as the light. Just then there appeared before them Moses and Elijah, talking with Jesus." Peter was so awestruck that he said, "Lord, it is good for us to be here. If you wish, I will put up three shelters—one for you, one for Moses and one for Elijah."[5]

After the resurrection of Christ. The New Testament writers record Jesus' appearance to his disciples and a gathering of five hundred people following his death and resurrection.

Then there is the intriguing reference made by the writer of Hebrews: "Since we are surrounded by such a great cloud of witnesses, let us throw off everything that hinders and the sin that so easily entangles, and let us run with perseverance the race marked out for us."[6] It seems that deceased saints can observe what is going on here—is it possible they could do more than observe? We don't know.

That calls to mind the words of respected university professor and theologian Gerard Reed, who was in deep grief from the loss of his beloved wife following a battle with cancer. This man, not given to displays of emotion, said with tear-filled eyes, "I believe in the communion of the saints." He meant that even though his wife had gone on to heaven, he was still enjoying meaningful communion with her. Following scriptural directives, he was not seeking out contact with her; he simply was aware of her periodic presence.

In our quest to be open and honest about our exploration of "supernatural" events, we will acknowledge that the idea of dead people appearing to the living is highly controversial. Skeptics often say, "What grief-stricken person, overwhelmed by emotion and perhaps sleep deprived, wouldn't *want* to see their deceased family member or friend in a happy state? It's a matter of *projection* or *wish fulfillment*, a handy trick played by the mind." In some cases, that is probably true. And some events may simply be coincidences rather than supernatural events. But it isn't so easy to explain away the hundreds of reported visitation experiences that occur each year—often by people who were themselves skeptical at one point.

It is not our intent here to sway your opinion, but simply to present the experiences of several people as honestly and accurately as possible. We encourage you to discern the truth with God's guidance.

17

Never Far Away

———— ✳ ————

After her brother's heartbreaking death,
Megan Garlow drew strength from
a surprising source—her brother.

"Max!" Chris said in his best Jim Carrey-Grinch voice, "Grab a bag and we'll come back for the rest. Of course, when I say 'we,' I mean 'you.'"

From behind the steering wheel of her brother's car, Megan laughed. Of course Megan had heard the line before—probably a hundred times—but she never tired of hearing Chris's rendition of his favorite movie lines.

Which was a good thing. It was the second weekend of July 2009 and the siblings had embarked on a road trip, driving five hundred miles from Kansas to Colorado for a friend's wedding, then driving home again the next day. Over the course of the weekend, Megan would hear many funny quips from her entertaining brother.

The day after the wedding, while driving home, their banter took a deeper turn. On a whim, Megan turned to Chris and said, "Let's plan your wedding! Tell me who you'd pick for your groomsmen."

It was Chris's turn behind the wheel and, as he drove, he began spouting off the names of nearly a dozen men, a combination of brothers, cousins, and close friends.

"Wow! I'm impressed!" Megan said, then teased, "You've got this all figured out. You're not sweet on anyone, are you?"

Chris, twenty-one, grinned and shook his head. "Nope. But it's easy to know who I'd choose to stand with me at my wedding. Each of these guys has had a huge impact on my life."

Megan and Chris had always been close. Best friends really. But this was a new side to her brother. She was fascinated. "Tell me more," she prompted.

Chris told her the things he most appreciated about his brother-in-law Caleb, brother Nathan, cousins Jimmie, Wes, and Josh, and friends Wes, Jameson, Jack, Scott, and Matt.

When she got home, Megan told her parents, Bill and Laurie Garlow, about her conversation with Chris. Looking forward to Chris's wedding one day, they wrote down the names of his future groomsmen.

Two weeks later, these men would serve as pallbearers at Chris's funeral.

On July 16, Chris's charred car was discovered in a supermarket parking lot with someone inside, burned beyond recognition. Authorities were still trying to identify the body, but there seemed little reason to believe the young man who had perished was anyone other than Chris Garlow.

If any accident could be called "freak," it was this one. Parking lot security cameras showed Chris's car pulling into the lot around

4:45 in the morning and stopping at the far end of the lot. The video showed that no one approached or got out of the car. A little later, smoke could be seen coming from the hood of the car, then flames engulfed the engine and spread rapidly.

The best explanation the authorities and the family have been able to piece together is this: Chris was on his way home early that morning after being with friends. His frequent struggles with insomnia meant he was normally awake past 3:00 a.m., at which time he would become profoundly tired. In addition, he had just begun taking new medication to assist with his allergies, and it might have affected his alertness. Extremely sleepy, and not wanting to get pulled over for weaving, he turned into the parking lot.

It was a warm night. Chris turned off the headlights but left the car running, along with the air-conditioner. He pushed his seat back and closed his eyes. He just needed a short nap and he'd be good to go. When the car overheated and the fire started in the engine block, Chris didn't wake up. He was overcome by fumes and later by flames. He probably never stirred at all.

Looking back, Megan and her family realized Chris's death might explain something that had happened years earlier. Chris and Megan's older brother, Robbie, who has Down syndrome, became very ill with altitude sickness during a family visit to Colorado. The situation became so serious that he had to be hospitalized. While there, he was sedated after having a tracheotomy tube inserted in his throat. At one point, he suddenly became agitated, then nearly hysterical. Over and over, he cried out, "Fire! Fire! Chris! Chris out! Fire!" Robbie kept pointing and yelling until Chris was brought to him so he could see that his little brother, then ten, was safe.

It seemed that Robbie had a premonition of his brother's death more than ten years before it happened.

In the months following Chris's funeral—officiated by his uncle Jim Garlow and attended by hundreds of grieving but grateful loved ones—his family continued trying to cope with their profound sadness. For Megan, preserving precious memories of Chris became extremely important. She spent most of the summer making photo collages of Chris and writing letters to his closest friends—the men he'd identified for groomsmen, the same ones who had carried his casket—recounting for them the wonderful things Chris had told her about each of them days before his death.

One of Megan's most enjoyable memories of Chris was the road trip they took together to Colorado. Her most poignant memory, however, was of the final evening of a Fourth of July family camping trip shortly before Chris died.

Bill and Laurie had taken all six kids RV camping and one night around the campfire, as often happens, the enveloping darkness and mesmerizing flames inspired meaningful conversation. Someone brought up the book their uncle Jim had just written with coauthor Keith Wall titled *Heaven and the Afterlife,* and the discussion turned to many provocative subjects. As various family members shared their thoughts and feelings about a range of topics—including near-death experiences, angels, demons, heaven, and hell—it was a bittersweet reminder that their precious years together on earth were temporary. It was also a reminder that, because of their Christian faith, the separation would be temporary, and one day the family would be reunited for eternity in heaven. Looking around the circle of fire-lit faces of people she loved, Megan couldn't imagine life without any of them. And yet eleven days later Chris would be gone.

That fall, Megan moved to Colorado to begin a career as a high school teacher. The start of the school year kept her busier than she could have imagined. Still, the ache was there, and she missed Chris more than she could express.

And Megan still had a pressing question. She wanted to know what Chris's life was like *now*. Over and over again, she wrote in her journal, "Chris, where are you? What's it like where you are now? What's heaven *really* like?"

One night she dreamed about her brother.

It wasn't the same dream she'd been having for weeks, where Chris was hanging out with her family and then suddenly disappeared. Every time she had that dream, Megan awoke with the heart-sickening realization that, yes, Chris was truly gone forever.

This time she dreamed she was with her mother and her sisters Brooke and Amanda. The four women were laughing and reminiscing about the things they loved most about Chris.

"Remember how he always quoted funny movie lines?" Brooke said.

Amanda added, "Remember how Dad would always say to him, 'How can you remember *that* stuff and you can't remember the stuff you need to know for your tests at school?'"

The other women smiled fondly.

Suddenly, just to the right of where her mother sat, Megan saw her brother's face begin to materialize, and then his body. He was laughing right along with them, as if he'd been listening in and just now decided to make his presence known. He looked just like, well . . . Chris. He was tall and tan with brown hair and mischievous brown eyes.

"Chris!" Megan cried out.

He assured the women it was really him and, when Megan wasn't so sure, he took her hand and placed it on his arm. Despite the fact that he was still somewhat transparent, Chris's arm felt solid to the touch.

Megan realized this was her chance. "Chris," she said breathlessly, "tell me about heaven."

His faced glowed. "It's awesome and beautiful beyond words.

And people are themselves. They still look like themselves, and they have their same personalities."

Megan and her sisters exchanged glances. "So Brooke will still be Brooke? And Amanda will still be Amanda?"

"Exactly!" Chris said. "And everyone has jobs. Not like the jobs here, where people are often bored or unhappy. Everyone loves their jobs there. In some ways it's like earth, but everyone is happier."

One of the sisters asked, "What's your job, Chris?"

"Oh, I haven't found one yet."

The women laughed. Apparently, heaven really *was* just like earth for their happy-go-lucky brother.

Chris caught their drift and grinned, "Now, hold on a minute. It's not like that. The reason I don't have a job yet is because right now I'm staying pretty busy looking out for my friends and family. And there are a lot of you guys, so it takes up most of my time. Plus I guess I'm not ready to leave you all behind quite yet and be fully committed there—"

And that's when Megan woke up. But for the first time since the accident, she awakened with an overwhelming feeling of peace.

A few months later, in January, Megan sat in a plane, flying home to Kansas to visit her family. After the crew had made their announcements and everyone had settled in for the flight, Megan reached for a book she'd just purchased titled *Heaven*. The author, Randy Alcorn, had based his findings on twenty-five years of research. As she began to read, Megan discovered that Alcorn's portrait of heaven included none of the stereotypical images of clouds and harps. Instead, she read about a place much like earth, only perfected . . . a place where beauty abounded and people had personalities and even purpose.

Suddenly she was struck by the thought that nothing she read sounded new to her at all.

Heaven, as Alcorn portrayed it, is exactly the way Chris had described it to Megan in her dream two months after he died.

Megan put the book down. She looked out the window, overcome with peace and something else too. What she felt was gratitude.

Staring out over the magical landscape of clouds, she thanked God for Chris, for the life Chris was experiencing even now in heaven . . . and for the answers and comfort Chris had been allowed to give her.

Chris's family will be the first to admit that on the bad days it feels like Chris is gone forever. It's an overwhelming sense of loss. But on the good days it's a little easier to remember what they've come to understand with all their hearts: Chris hasn't stopped existing, but is merely someplace else. The separation—although painful—is temporary. And most of all, one day the Garlow family reunion in heaven will be worth the wait.

18

A Bond Between Brothers

After his brother drowned, Juan Valdivia was
given extra time to say good-bye.

On a particularly beautiful spring day—May 12, 1992—Juan Valdivia could
see blue sky and bright sun outside the window of his Sacramento office.
He'd recently finished the classroom portion of his training to become a
legal clerk and had landed a promising job at a local law firm. His wife,
Cindy, and their three kids were healthy and happy. Life was good.

Then he got the phone call. Cindy was on the other end of the
line.

"Joe is missing," she said. "The prison called to say he never
showed up for work this morning."

Time stood still in Juan's tiny office when he heard those words.
The spring sunshine pouring through the glass suddenly lost its warmth,

and a chill went through his body. Joe was his older brother–though, in truth, Juan thought of him as more of a father. As a teenager, he had even lived with Joe in Germany for a time, while his brother was in the military and stationed there.

These days, Joe worked as a prison inspector at the Mule Creek State Prison in Ione, California, an hour-long commute from his home in Sacramento. Joe left home every workday between four and five o'clock in the morning.

"You have to understand something about Joe," Juan said. "He was the kind of guy who'd show up for work early, leave late, and not take a lunch break. He was regular and reliable like a clock. So for him not to show up for work was a big deal. We knew immediately that something was not right."

Juan headed straight home when he hung up the phone, while another brother, Eddie, and Joseph, Joe's son, began retracing Joe's probable route to work that morning. At home, Juan sat helplessly on the couch in his living room with a cold feeling of dread whipping around him like a winter wind. Though it wasn't like him to feel chilly, that day he wrapped himself in a blanket and waited for news.

It didn't take long for the phone to ring again. Eddie and Joseph had found Joe's cream-colored Chevy Blazer beside a wide, concrete-lined aqueduct where it crossed Florin Road in southeast Sacramento. The hood stood open, and the cap was off the radiator. The engine was running–just as it had been for at least ten hours. Police were on the scene now and had begun to search the water, which was ten feet deep and flowing rapidly southward to the farmland of the San Joaquin Valley.

"I wanted to jump in my car right then and drive out to the canal and help look for my brother," Juan said. "I felt useless doing anything else. But we decided to go to my mom's house instead and wait there, in case the worst had happened."

The entire family bristled with anxious energy–and dread. It had already been a hard year for Joe and his wife and kids. A few months earlier, he'd been shot in the legs by a stranger, for no better reason than the fact that the man wanted the San Francisco 49ers jacket Joe wore. After massive surgery and lengthy physical therapy, Joe was left with several pins and rods in his legs that caused him constant pain.

And now this. Juan could hardly believe it was really happening.

The phone rang once more, and their last sliver of hope was shattered. Authorities found Joe's body—a quarter mile from where his truck sat—pinned by the rushing water to a metal grate designed to catch brush and other debris. He'd been dead since early that morning.

———

After the funeral, Juan was plagued by a swarm of conflicting feelings. He was confused by the many unanswered questions concerning Joe's death. He felt betrayed and abandoned by his brother—and then felt guilty for his selfishness. Juan endured devastating grief along with the overwhelming sense of responsibility to care for the family Joe left behind—his wife and four kids. Most of all, he was angry at God.

"I had only been a Christian a couple of years, and I didn't know anything about going to heaven or hell," he said. "Like lots of people, I had questions, but no answers. I didn't really give the afterlife that much thought."

Exactly one week after burying Joe, Juan was seized by the urge to drive out to the canal where Joe had died. He hadn't been there yet, not fully trusting his fragile emotions to hold up. But that day he was compelled to go, as if he had no choice in the matter. He went to remember and reflect—and grieve the father figure he had lost.

He parked his car beside the canal fence, which was newly patched and secured so no one else could climb down to the water. He got out, crossed to the passenger side, and sat on the hood. The afternoon sun was headed toward the horizon, bathing the wide-open fields all around him in a golden glow. He looked out over the aqueduct, his mind a torrent of motion, like the water below, full of painful questions. A deep silence settled around him.

"Hey, Johnny, what are you doing here?"

Joe's voice came from the direction of the setting sun. There was no mistaking it for someone else. When alive, Joe always called Juan "Johnny."

Juan glanced toward the sound and saw his brother's silhouette, backlit by the sunlight, coming toward him. At first, Joe looked indistinct, like a shadow. But the closer he came, the more real and solid he appeared. By the time he came to a stop just a few feet from Juan's car, Joe looked as substantial as any living person. Juan heard his voice just as clearly too.

"It sounds strange now," Juan recalled, "but I wasn't scared or surprised at all to see him there. I hadn't gone out there expecting anything like that to happen. But once he was standing there, it all seemed so natural."

Joe was wearing the formal Department of Corrections dress uniform he'd been buried in. Juan's eyes were drawn to the flash of a gold pin in the shape of the letter "J" on the lapel of his jacket—right where Juan had put it when he leaned over his brother's casket a week earlier to say one last good-bye. It had been a Christmas gift from Joe the previous year.

His brother looked good—healthy and alive. His skin was clear and fairer than it had been. There was a soft angelic light around him.

"Johnny, what are you doing here?" he asked.

Juan calmly explained that he just needed some answers. He wanted to see where Joe had gone into the water and find out what had happened.

Juan looked at the figure standing before him. "Did you suffer?"

"No, I didn't suffer," Joe answered. "When the truck overheated I tried to get some water from the aqueduct. I slipped on the algae at the edge of the water and hit my head. It knocked me out, but I didn't feel anything."

Then Juan's brother explained: Pulled immediately under the surface, Joe then saw a hand and arm reach down and take hold of him. It pulled him upward out of the water. Joe glanced back down and saw his body drift away in the murky current. When he looked around for the person who'd lifted him up, there was no one to be seen.

He knew then that he was dead—and felt an amazing sense of peace and well-being. He told Juan he visited everyone in the family after that, to say good-bye—though without being seen by anyone. He attended the funeral and was proud of the way the family came together and supported each other, even in their pain and grief.

"He repeated to me parts of conversations I'd had with the family that day," Juan said. "He described what our mother was wearing—and laughed because she'd had on two different shoes. Nobody else noticed that."

Joe knew that Juan had been upset on the day of the funeral because his mother had invited a troupe of Aztec dancers in native dress to perform during the ceremonies—without consulting the rest of the family. He advised Juan to let it go and accept it as a necessary part of their mother's grieving process.

Joe talked about how long they'd had to wait at the cemetery for the last cars in the funeral procession to finally arrive.

"He thanked me for not taking the freeway," Juan remembered with a smile. "That was something he always hated when he was alive. We took the back roads, and even though we had twenty-two motorcycle escorts, it still wasn't enough."

Joe asked Juan to watch over his kids and keep them out of trouble.

Then Juan broke down and revealed how he felt about being abandoned by the brother he depended on for so much. Everything Juan knew about being a father and a man, he'd learned from Joe—and there was so much more to know.

"How could you leave me?" he asked.

"It was my time," Joe replied matter-of-factly. "I had no choice. But things are amazing here. And I don't have any more pain."

Suddenly, Joe said it was time for Juan to go home, before Cindy got worried. He began to walk away in the direction from which he had come. Juan slid off the hood of the car and walked to the driver's side door. By the time he got there, Joe was gone. Forty-five minutes had gone by.

———

Shortly after this encounter, Juan made a major change in his life. He left the legal profession and became a mortician.

"What I went through with Joe made me intensely curious about the whole death process," he said. "I wanted to know what happens to bodies when we die, how an autopsy works, and so on. It definitely gave me a huge amount of compassion for people who have suffered a loss. Even after eighteen years in this business, it is more than just a job to me. I still get emotional when helping a family who has just lost someone."

And the experience has matured and strengthened Juan's faith in God.

"I know for sure that God's angels are watching over us and that death is not an end. It's a beginning," he said. "I believe Joe is about the Father's business now, just like Jesus said."

———

Weeks after his visit with Joe, Juan sat looking through the photos taken at the funeral. In one, Joe's wife, Erlinda, is seated next to his mother at the graveside. Since Joe was a veteran of the armed forces, Erlinda is reaching out to receive a folded flag from a uniformed member of the honor guard. But that's not what caught Juan's attention. Instead, his eyes were drawn to his mother's feet.

He grinned when he saw that she wore two shoes, both of the same style—but one brown and the other black.

19

"You've Come Back!"

After the death of her husband, Norma
Knudson's sagging spirits were lifted when
she was visited by his spirit.

Late one evening, Norma Knudson reclined on the sofa in the living
room of her comfortable San Diego home. An open book lay in her
hands. Her eyes moved as if reading the words, and she turned the
page at appropriate intervals—but her mind was elsewhere. Or perhaps
it was simply nowhere, a foggy place where all her senses had gone
numb, where time seemed to inch along like a mountain glacier. Some
nights she turned on the TV and stared blankly at the screen, watching
the images, but never really seeing them.

   She was an old woman, about to turn eighty—on April Fool's Day.
Anyone who saw her sitting there, staring vacantly at her book, might
have chalked up her lethargy to simple fatigue or a mind gone slack

with age. But that would have been incorrect. Her problem wasn't old age or slipping mental faculties—it was deep depression.

Norma suffered from *grief*.

Just two months earlier, Curt, her husband and devoted partner of fifty years, had died in the bedroom just a few steps from the sofa where she rested. After an exhausting and emotionally trying year, Curt succumbed to a rare condition called Lewy body disease, a little-known cousin to Alzheimer's and Parkinson's diseases. Lewy bodies (named for their discoverer, Frederick Lewy) are microscopic protein deposits that form in nerve cells in the brain, disrupting normal function. There is presently no cure, and the debilitating symptoms—increasing dementia, loss of motor control, and a progressive inability to communicate—all advance rapidly after they first appear.

"I am a strong person; I know that," Norma recalled. "I cared for both my aunt and my father for years toward the end of their lives. But this was almost more than I could take. I cared for Curt almost by myself. My daughter helped, of course, but she was busy running her own business. He couldn't swallow well and wouldn't eat what I made for him. Worse, he couldn't tell me what he did want. I loved him dearly, but I have to admit I got angry and frustrated at times."

Being suddenly unable to communicate with Curt was the hardest part for Norma. They had been best friends for all those years together. Talking and laughing with each other and Hanna, their only daughter, was as much a vital part of their lives as the food they ate and the air they breathed. Before he died, Curt could no longer express his most basic needs, much less carry on the sort of conversation Norma had so enjoyed. He looked blankly back at her when she tried to tell him how she felt or what the doctors said when they finally diagnosed his condition correctly.

For months, Norma had done nothing but care for Curt. Gone were the frequent strolls down Grand Avenue to the stretch of Pacific beach they had marveled at together for years. Also gone was time to spend on her work as an artist. Tending to her beloved husband had consumed her life and depleted her energy.

After the funeral, her physical and emotional exhaustion caught up with her—and she withdrew even more deeply behind the drawn shades and closed doors of her house.

"I cried a lot," she said. "Everything in the house reminded me of him. Nothing seemed worthwhile without him there to share it."

So that night, when she lay on the sofa attempting to read a book, it was just another evening in the flat landscape her life had become. The gray house cat, Boogie—an abused stray Curt had rescued from a life on the streets two years earlier—climbed onto Norma's chest and settled in for a nap. Soon, Norma fell asleep as well, too tired to move to the bedroom. The only sounds in the house were the hum of the refrigerator in the kitchen and Boogie's soft purring.

A short time later, a sharp pain piercing her chest jolted Norma awake. Boogie had suddenly jumped up and scratched her as he darted away down the hall toward the bathroom. Norma's first thought as she rubbed her clawed skin was one of irritation at the cat. But it took only a second to forget about that and to realize something was very, very different.

She heard a sound coming from down the hall. Water was running loudly in the bathroom shower.

Then she smelled the floral scent of soap and shampoo.

And then . . . could it be? Curt's booming, beautiful singing voice filled the house, just the way it used to whenever he took a shower.

"Oh my, you've come back!" Norma cried, as waves of relief and comfort washed over her. Time not only seemed to stand still, it practically vanished altogether. "I am so glad you are home!"

Boogie returned from the bathroom and began running around the house, frantically excited, his raccoon-like black-and-gray ringed tail waving like a flag.

"Oh, I am so glad you are home!"

But wait, Norma thought as she remembered the events of the past several months. *I must be dreaming. He couldn't have come home. This is not real.*

She looked toward the bathroom. The sound of water splashing seemed real enough. Curt, a professional musician and music teacher in his younger days, was belting out a song he'd sung so often while living—Tennessee Ernie Ford's classic tune:

> You load sixteen tons what do you get
> Another day older and deeper in debt
> Saint Peter don't you call me 'cause I can't go
> I owe my soul to the company store

"I know what I heard, and I certainly *felt* wide awake," Norma recalled later. "I had the red, stinging cat scratches to prove it. But I still didn't believe it."

She went to the kitchen to put on a pot of coffee and "straighten herself out." The comforting aroma helped settle her mind. When she returned to the living room, the shower was still running. Her deceased husband was still singing. She sat down gingerly on the sofa to collect herself.

Then suddenly the sound of cascading water stopped—and Curt strode into the room, beaming with energy and presence. He sat down beside Norma in his favorite chair, smiling and laughing. The achingly familiar scent of the cologne he wore when alive—*Allure Homme* by Chanel—filled the air. Though he died at age seventy-nine, Norma was astonished to see him as he had looked when he was a handsome "youngster" of thirty-five. His skin was young and supple, his hair curly and brown. Curt wore clothes Norma had never seen before—a crisp white shirt with blue stripes under a tan jacket. He had on tan trousers and shiny brown loafers.

"He looked *great,*" Norma said later. "He looked like a million bucks!"

The disbelief she had felt moments ago evaporated and she said to him again and again, "You're home! I'm so glad you came home!"

"Yes," Curt said to her warmly. "I'm fine, I'm good! Don't worry."

The sound of his voice was pure music to Norma's ears. Weeks before he died, Curt had lost the ability to speak. It was devastating to soul mates like them who talked to each other all the time about everything. They conversed on long walks, during dinner, before sleep at night. They had no secrets and indulged in no brooding silences. Now there he was talking to her, after she'd given up on ever hearing his voice again.

"You look wonderful," she said.

"I am!" he replied with a smile that seemed to stretch from ear to ear. "Everything is wonderful."

"I can see you, but I know I can't touch you," Norma said, thinking that *must* be one of the rules when you are visited by your deceased husband, no matter how strongly his cologne fills the room.

His smile broadened. "Oh yes, you can," he said, playfully.

He held out his hand to her. Without hesitation, she took it. His skin was soft and alive—and very real.

"His hand was warm, almost hot," Norma remembered. "We held hands like that for quite some time and just looked at each other. He smiled, and looked so wonderful and healthy. I couldn't believe my eyes."

"Don't worry," Curt said again. "Everything is fine."

Then he slowly disappeared from sight, like a movie that gradually fades at the end. After a few moments, Boogie jumped into the chair where Curt had been seated and, at last, sat still.

What in the world just happened to me? Norma thought, without a trace of fear. On the contrary, she felt like shouting and dancing. She went to the kitchen and poured a cup of coffee, glad to have something familiar to do with her shaking hands. Even there, his scent was still powerfully present. An idea suddenly crossed her mind, and she practically ran to the bathroom to see if the shower was wet.

It was dry.

She checked the medicine cabinet in case the last bottle of Curt's cologne had fallen over and spilled.

No, it hadn't.

"I drank coffee the rest of the night," she said with a laugh. "I couldn't possibly sleep. I know he came back to tell me that everything was okay, that I should stop worrying and grieving so much."

And that's exactly what she did.

"Since my husband came to visit, my life has turned around completely," she said. "I still walk around the house and I see things that remind me of him, but now it's okay. I've seen for myself that he is well where he is, and I'm not afraid. I know we'll see each other again."

Norma no longer spends her evenings in a fog of depression, staring blankly at the television, or at books she can't remember reading. She's painting again—creating lovely portraits, her specialty. She's cooking once more, enjoying the flavors she had all but forgotten during Curt's illness and after his death. And every morning she takes a long walk on the beach.

Occasionally, Norma's house still fills with the scent of *Allure Homme*, but she no longer checks the bathroom medicine chest for a spill. She just smiles and thanks God for the comfort it brings.

"Now I have absolutely no fear of death," she said. "It's just a continuation of living."

20

1127

—— ✳ ——

After her dad died, Hanna Sheldon found
comfort in an unexpected place.

Hanna Sheldon turned out the lights in her office at the Pine Hills
Lodge and was surprised at how feeble the late-afternoon light was
that fell through the window. The rain that threatened to spill from
low-hanging clouds all day had finally followed through, coloring the
surrounding Cuyamaca Mountains a heavy, foreboding shade of gray.
The lodge–Hanna's labor of love for the past several years–was a rustic
but elegant resort in the historic mining town of Julian, California.

Today as she ran through the storm to her car for the ninety-minute
trip home to San Diego, Hanna felt as dark and dull on the inside as
the world looked outside. In truth, a deluge of tears had been steadily
gathering throughout the day along with the rain. She shut the car

door behind her, looked at her drenched appearance in the rearview mirror, and knew it was going to be a long ride home.

In all the years she'd been making the trip to the lodge, she had never grown tired of the beautiful scenery—rolling mountains, lush apple orchards, and forests of oak, cedar, and pine. But three months ago, all that changed. Something happened to drain the joy out of Hanna's life and wrap her in a suffocating depression.

Her father died.

After a year of progressively losing his ability to walk, eat, and communicate, Curt Knudson died of Lewy body disease, a rare brain ailment akin to Parkinson's and Alzheimer's (see Norma Knudson's story in the previous chapter). He had been a wonderful father to Hanna—involved, fun-loving, and caring. Letting go of him had been the hardest thing she had ever been called upon to do. She'd begun to doubt whether her life would ever regain its luster.

As she pulled her car onto the winding highway and headed toward home, Hanna began to cry. She let loose and gave up on trying to be brave and controlled. She cried and cried. And she verbalized all of her feelings, as if her father were seated in the seat beside her.

"I'm sure I looked like a crazy woman, crying and talking out loud to nobody," she recalled. "But I didn't care who saw me. There weren't many people on the road that day anyway, though it wouldn't have mattered. After carrying so much emotion, I was ready to unload."

And she did. She "opened a vein," as creative types say, and let her blood and guts spill out. She had no typical unfinished business with her dad—no confessions to make, no forgiveness to ask or give. Mostly she wanted to express how sorry she was that his condition had been misdiagnosed for so long during the year he was in decline. Improper medication had contributed to his dramatic loss of normal mental and physical function.

She poured out all the things she'd been unable to say to him in the last weeks and months of his life, as his ability to communicate became more sporadic and impaired. Though she was uttering words in a car occupied only by herself, she sensed she wasn't alone. She thanked her father for the recent miraculous after-death visit he'd made to her mother and told him how much that had meant to both of them.

She remembered something then, something very significant: the number 1127. And she wondered if this sign would appear again. On that day, when her emotions were raw and her tears ran, she earnestly hoped so.

Why 1127? A few weeks before anyone in the family knew Curt's gradually failing health was serious, Hanna began to wake up unexpectedly at night. She would glance at the digital clock across the room. Each time it would display exactly the same time—11:27.

It happened during the day as well.

"I'm not a person who is obsessed with the time," Hanna explained. "I rarely look at clocks. But something suddenly started happening a lot: when I did look at a clock, it would say 11:27. That really got my attention. It made me think I needed to spend more time with my parents and to more actively help find out what was wrong with Dad."

How could four simple numbers communicate all that to Hanna? The answer lies in the address of the home where her parents had lived for many decades: 1127 Grand Avenue, San Diego, California.

As unorthodox as the experience was, Hanna decided she must act on the message she was receiving. Running Pine Hills Lodge had kept her from seeing Curt and Norma as often as she once did. But over the following year, she became much more involved in helping them cope with her father's encroaching illness. When he could no longer drive, she took him to doctor appointments and on other errands. She spent hours helping her mother deal with Curt's daily care. Throughout this time, it became a common occurrence for her to see 11:27 on clocks everywhere she went—sometimes at random times of the day when the clock *shouldn't* say 11:27.

Hanna was present when Curt died in his own bed. His passing was peaceful, his daughter holding one of his hands and his wife holding the other.

The very next night she woke up—at 11:27. In the weeks after her father's funeral, she saw 11:27 even more often. It was on the microwave, on the clock on her computer, just about anywhere there was a digital time display.

"I tried to tell myself it was all in my head," she said. "But it really did feel like my dad was trying to comfort me."

Then came the tearful day she drove from Julian to San Diego, months after her dad's death, when she found herself talking out loud to her empty car as she navigated rain-slicked streets. She had so hoped for another sign that he was okay. By the time she arrived home, she felt strangely refreshed after crying so hard and pouring out her heart.

Several days later, around 3:30 in the afternoon, Hanna was busy checking the empty cabins at the lodge before heading home for the day. She was making sure the heaters and lights were off, no water was left running, and the doors were securely locked. Toward the end of her rounds, she stepped into "Pine Cone One," a cozy 1920s-era cabin—the only one her parents ever stayed in when they visited Pine Hills.

The room was dark—the curtains were drawn and the lights were off. In the shadows, a flashing yellow light caught Hanna's attention. She turned toward it and saw the digital clock on the table blinking on and off, the way they do after a power outage, a common occurrence in the mountains. That day, the tiny display might as well have been a neon billboard at Times Square as it repeatedly flashed:

11:27 . . . 11:27 . . . 11:27 . . .

"First, I laughed out loud," Hanna recalled. "Then I sat down on the bed and cried. It is hard to describe, but the whole atmosphere in the room changed. The air felt warmer and heavier somehow. Everything seemed to be moving in slow motion. I was certain he was right there with me, and I sat there for what seemed like a very long time just saying, 'Thank you, Daddy' over and over. It was such a beautiful, comforting feeling."

Then the flashing numbers on the clock changed to 11:28, and the moment passed. She had received the message she had hoped for. And it became the turning point in her process of grief and healing.

"Now when I think of him, I have such a grateful, happy feeling," she said. "I'm not so sad anymore. This is exactly the sort of thing he would do, so fun and playful and creative."

Hanna still sees 1127 appearing at odd times every now and then—and it always brings a smile to her face and comfort to her heart.

21

A Gift Like No Other

———— ✳ ————

With an illness more serious than physicians
thought, Miranda Zorn's life was likely
saved—by a deceased friend.

"Mom, we should see ourselves in a mirror!" Miranda said with a laugh. "We're covered in powdered sugar."

It was December 18, 2004, and Miranda Zorn was home from college on winter break. Decorating cookies with her mom, Phyllis Zorn, in the sunny kitchen in their home, in Ellis, Kansas, Miranda felt like Christmas had finally arrived.

The banter between the two women was lively and warm as the cookies took shape. A few days earlier, a neighbor had given them a hand-painted Christmas plate piled high with home-baked goodies, and Miranda and Phyllis were making cookies so they could reciprocate.

Sliding another batch of snowballs out of the oven, Miranda's thoughts flew back in time ten years as she found herself remembering another neighbor who had been a cherished part of her life. In fact, Mary had been much more than a neighbor. The mother of Miranda's best friend, Mary was like a second mom to Miranda and her brother, and like a sister to Phyllis. The two families had done everything together. And while it was hard not to think of Mary at Christmastime, it was impossible today—the anniversary of her death.

On this day nine years earlier, Mary had died unexpectedly after a brief illness, leaving behind four of her own devastated children, plus Miranda and her brother, Ben, as well.

Arranging the cooled cookies on a plate, Miranda turned to her mother. "I remember how Mary always doubled the recipes so we could bake one batch of cookies and eat the other batch raw," she said. "And remember when the car broke down? She made sure we had groceries, drove us to school, then drove you all around town to shop for another car."

Phyllis smiled wistfully. "She always did take good care of us."

It was impossible to talk about Mary Frederick without feeling a sense of delight. At 6' 3" with long red hair and freckles, Mary stood out in a crowd. But the most memorable feature had been her vivacious spirit. When she died of a staph infection, it had been a huge blow to everyone who loved her. To make matters worse, there had been little warning. A case of pneumonia had gone awry and within thirty-six hours Mary was dead at age thirty-four.

A few days after making cookies with her mom, Miranda developed a cold, then a sore throat. On Christmas morning, despite waking up to the smell of cinnamon rolls and coffee, she groaned and pulled the covers up tight around her neck. Her throat still felt raw, and pressure still filled her sinuses. But now her ears hurt too.

The next day, when Miranda began feeling nauseous in addition to everything else, Phyllis bundled her daughter into the car and drove her to the ER. Miranda was diagnosed with a virus, given a steroid shot to boost her immune system, and sent home to recuperate.

Instead of feeling better, however, Miranda felt increasingly fatigued. Two days later, she complained that the spot on her hip where she'd gotten the shot was not only tender, but red and inflamed as well.

"The nurse said it might get sore," Phyllis reminded her daughter. "But let's keep an eye on it."

On New Year's Eve, while getting dressed for a party, Miranda again complained about the tender place where she had received the shot. When Phyllis went to inspect, she let out a gasp.

The spot on Miranda's hip was no longer a pinkish nodule about the size of a dime. Now several inches in diameter, the mark looked angry and inflamed, dark red, and obviously very painful.

Alarmed, Phyllis snapped a picture of the affected skin on her cell phone and emailed it to their family doctor.

The next day, all Miranda could do was sleep. Exhausted and achy, she felt constantly nauseated. The injection site burned. By midafternoon, she was ready for her third nap of the day. Pulling on a T-shirt and a pair of pajama bottoms, she climbed into bed, pulled the covers up to her chest, closed her eyes, and began to pray.

Lord, I don't know what's wrong with me, but I'm scared that it's a lot more serious than any of us realize. Please help me. Please. . . .

While still praying, she felt the mattress shift as someone—probably her mother or brother—sat down on the bed beside her. Miranda opened her eyes. She blinked and stared.

The woman sitting on the bed with her was Mary.

She'd aged a little, the laugh lines on her face a little deeper, the hair at her temples starting to go gray, the rest of her red mane pulled up and back into a ponytail. Reaching over, she stroked Miranda's hair, tucking a wayward lock behind her ear.

"It's going to get worse before it gets better," she told Miranda. "But it's going to be okay. You're going to be all right."

Mary patted Miranda's face. Miranda closed her eyes and smiled. She felt a wave of warmth wash over her body. Feeling relaxed and at peace, she fell sound asleep.

She woke up a couple of hours later. Usually a restless sleeper, Miranda thought it odd that she woke up in the exact position she'd been in when she fell asleep, on her back with the covers pulled up to her chest. The only difference? A lock of Miranda's hair was tucked behind her ear, and there was still an indentation in the covers where Mary had sat.

Miranda climbed gingerly out of bed and hurried down the hall to find her mother. She found Phyllis at the kitchen table, drinking tea and reading a book.

"Mom!" she called out. "I just saw Mary!"

Phyllis looked up, startled.

Phyllis listened intently as Miranda told her what had happened. Mary's message had been clear: Miranda would get worse before she would get better. And yet Miranda's doctors weren't treating her illness very seriously. Realizing her daughter was in danger, Phyllis placed another call to the emergency room. It was time to get aggressive about finding Miranda the help she needed.

Back in the ER, Dr. Alan Adams examined Miranda. "It might be an acute allergic reaction, but it could also be an infection—possibly from receiving an injection with a dirty needle. I'm putting you on 2000 milligrams of antibiotics, and I want you to use hot compresses for the pain."

When Phyllis asked the doctor to take a culture to see exactly what the problem was, Dr. Adams advised doing the procedure at the right time, when the wound opened. Miranda's regular physician, meanwhile, continually resisted getting a culture, saying it was unnecessary.

The following weekend, the abscess on Miranda's hip burst open and began to drain. Phyllis called the ER and spoke with the doctor on call. She demanded he run a culture on the infected site, and this time she wouldn't take no for an answer.

Three days later, Phyllis and Miranda returned to the doctor's office to hear the results of the tests. But instead of being led into one of the exam rooms, they were ushered quickly down the hall into the office of an infectious-disease specialist.

The new doctor entered the room and greeted the two women. "What can I do for you today?" he asked with a smile.

Miranda sighed, in too much pain to bring the new guy up to speed. Phyllis filled him in and explained that they'd come for the results of Miranda's culture.

The doctor went to his computer and looked up Miranda's file. As he read the test results aloud, Phyllis's blood ran cold. Miranda's problem wasn't because of an allergic reaction after all. Miranda had an infection due to staphylococcus aureus. The doctor said he was going to operate and clean out the infected site immediately.

Miranda winced. "Do you have to? Can't I just take stronger antibiotics?"

Phyllis turned toward her daughter. "Miranda—" There was a sobering tone in her voice that drew Miranda's attention immediately. Phyllis said, "We don't have a choice. We can't have the same thing happen to you that happened to Mary."

As Phyllis looked on, understanding slowly dawned in Miranda's eyes. Understanding, and then awe. *"Mary?"*

Her mother nodded.

"It's the same kind of infection that killed Mary?"

Her mother nodded again.

At that moment, both women knew. The ever-protective second mom, Mary had visited Miranda in order to keep her from dying from the same illness that had claimed her own life nearly ten years earlier.

That afternoon, the doctor applied local anesthetic and made his incision to clean out the infection. He was shocked to realize the extent of the damage wreaked on Miranda's body by the bacteria. Staphylococcus aureas, when trapped under the surface of the skin, releases a toxin that destroys surrounding tissue, turning it into liquid. The amount of liquefied tissue that needed to be removed created a wound the width of a person's hand and several inches deep. Other than the local anesthetic, the surgery had been performed without anything to numb the pain. To make matters worse, the resulting wound had to be cleaned and repacked with gauze every day for weeks—another painful process.

In the ensuing days, Miranda was too consumed with healing to think much about her visit from Mary. Then one morning, several weeks into her recovery, she was eating breakfast and flipping channels on the TV when she came across a documentary on ghosts. She paused, TV remote in hand, as a wave of emotions came crashing in on her.

"I've always believed we wouldn't go through what we go through here on earth if there wasn't an afterlife, and Mary's visit is proof," she reflected. "Now I know there's more to life than just what we can see here on earth. God often sends help in ways we would never expect—sometimes in truly miraculous ways."

Three years later, Miranda had lunch with Leslie, one of Mary's four daughters. Before Mary visited Miranda, it had been years since the girls had even seen each other. Since Mary's visit, the girls—who live three hours apart—had been making the effort to meet halfway for an occasional late-afternoon lunch at Cinnamon's Deli.

Halfway through the meal, Miranda took a deep breath and said,

"Leslie, I know I've shared with you about the time, three years ago, when I got really sick. But there's a part of the story I've never told you, because I didn't know how it would impact you."

Leslie raised her brows. "Impact *me*?"

"Yes, you or even your sisters," Miranda said. "Because . . . because it has to do with your mom."

Miranda shared her story again, except this time she told the whole story, leaving nothing out. By the time she was finished, Leslie's cheeks were streaked with tears.

"I was ten when she died," Leslie said. "I've missed her so much. If she can come to you like that, why not me? Why hasn't she come to see me?" A wave of conflicting emotions crossed Leslie's face. Then, almost as quickly as it came, it was gone. She softened. "I'm glad she's all right. I've wondered so many times how she's doing. Now I don't have to worry that she's stuck in limbo or something. Now I know she's okay and that she can still watch over us sometimes."

Miranda had tears in her eyes as well. "Honey, I don't know why she came to me and not you. Maybe she knows it would be too hard for you or for her. Or maybe I was so close to dying myself she knew she had to intervene. I don't know. But I do know that she sees you, Leslie, and your sisters too. I also know I couldn't have gone through what I did without her words to hang onto."

Mary's visit was a gift of life for Miranda and a gift of hope for others who loved her and miss her still. Nearly ten years after her death, a woman known for being protective and generous found a way, yet again, to impact the lives of those she loved.

22

When Grandpa Said Good-bye

———— ✳ ————

For Jennifer Mizicko's family, the final farewell
wasn't so final.

Jennifer turned in the cushioned chair and tried to find a more comfortable position. As hospital waiting rooms went, this one wasn't bad—furnished more like a living room than the cold, sterile rooms in some medical facilities. But still, she and her family had spent many long hours here, sitting, praying, holding vigil, and waiting for the heartbreaking news that Ron was really gone.

Ron Wallace was Jennifer's stepfather, and at fifty-three he seemed a young candidate for myelodysplastic syndrome, the rare bone marrow disorder that would soon claim his life. Four months earlier, he had begun the tedious and lengthy process of receiving a bone marrow transplant in the hope of staving off the disease. But when a freak infection spread to his brain, he was transferred from the cancer ward to ICU. His family was notified: It wouldn't be much longer now.

It was night, and Jennifer wished she could find a way to fall asleep in the waiting room. She was so tired. She closed her eyes. She actually began to drift into a restless sleep.

Suddenly she was awakened by flickering lights. She opened her eyes. The bright overhead lights were glowing solidly, without a flicker in sight. She thought to herself, *Maybe I'm seeing angels*.

She tried to fall asleep several more times, but every time she got close to crossing over into slumber, she was aroused by flickering lights before her eyes. Finally she sat up and looked at her sister, Laura, who was also wide awake.

"You can't sleep either, huh?" Jennifer asked.

Laura said, "Every time I fall asleep I see angels flying around the room and lights flashing."

Jennifer stared at her sister a full minute before responding. "Really? That's strange. And you know what's even stranger? I keep seeing the same thing."

Ron had come into their lives nineteen years earlier when he married their mother. He had been a good stepfather to Carol's four daughters. He had been an even more amazing grandfather to his fifteen grandchildren. He was the kind of grandpa who was forever taking one of the kids fishing, to the park, or out for ice cream.

The night passed slowly. Around daybreak, a doctor approached the family and said it was just a matter of time. They took Ron off the ventilator and began allowing family members into his room to say their good-byes.

Jennifer and her sisters discussed whether or not to let their children in the room to say good-bye to their grandfather. Jennifer's eight-year-old son, Chris, and Laura's four-year-old daughter, Kira, wanted desperately to see Grandpa Ron one more time before he died. But the skin on Ron's face was turning black as the tissue began to die—something that can happen in the last hours of life—plus he was unconscious, so he couldn't have said anything to the children. In the end, the sisters decided that the disease had so ravaged Ron's body that his grandchildren would be better off not seeing him in his final hours.

And so the children stayed with relatives in the waiting room. They were nearby—the waiting room happened to be adjacent to Ron's room in ICU—and that would have to do.

In the final hours of her stepdad's life, Jennifer thought about the flickering lights she and Laura had seen each time they'd started to doze. She looked into the space above the bed where her stepfather lay dying. The air seemed empty, but was it really? Were angels there? Angels that could be glimpsed in the twilight between consciousness and sleep? Angels that had congregated in the thin space between life and death?

Ron died around four o'clock that afternoon. The girls cried and tried to comfort their mother, Carol.

About ten minutes later, Jennifer headed toward the waiting room to let Ron's grandkids know that he was gone.

As she walked into the room, Chris jumped up and ran to his mother. "Mom, Grandpa just died," he blurted.

Jennifer nodded. "He did. How did you know?"

"A few minutes ago I was getting tired so I sat down and started falling asleep, and just as I did, Grandpa came to me in a dream and told me he loved me and would miss me, but it was time for him to go to heaven. And, Mom, there were angels all around Grandpa, and they were singing this really amazing song. Then Grandpa waved to me, and I woke up."

Jennifer's husband, Mike, joined them as Chris finished telling his mom about his dream. No one else knew about Chris's experience.

So when another grandchild had the same dream that night, the family took note.

It was four-year-old Kira this time. She awoke on the morning after Ron's death singing a song. When her mother asked what she was singing, Kira said simply, "Grandpa was in my dream. He told me he loved me, but he was going to live in heaven and he would see me again one day. And there were angels everywhere and they were singing this song." Kira began to sing again and, indeed, sang that song for several weeks.

Kira and Chris had begged to be in the room with their grandpa when he died. Instead, they'd been in the waiting room. Is that why Ron appeared to them? To comfort them in their grief and disappointment at being so close yet not being allowed into the ICU? Or perhaps their senses had been sharpened as they waited in the same room where Jennifer and Laura had already sensed the presence of angels.

A third child had taken Ron's death particularly hard. Five-year-old Ashlee lived with her mother in a house they had shared with Grandpa Ron. She had loved her grandpa so much she had shaved her head during his illness out of solidarity and support. One night, about a week after Ron had died, Ashlee got out of bed to go to the bathroom, which was next to the room that had belonged to her grandfather when he was alive. Still aching at his absence, Ashlee walked slowly down the hallway and past his room. The hallway was dimly lit, the only light coming from a night-light in the bathroom. So Ashlee walked gingerly with her head down, watching her feet to avoid stumbling. Suddenly she walked into someone and fell backward, landing in a sitting position on the floor. Looking up, she saw her grandpa.

"Ashlee, what are you doing up?"

"Grandpa! What are you doing here? They said you died!"

Her grandpa squatted down so he could look her in the eyes. "I just came to check on you, and tell you that I love you." He smiled and nodded toward Ashlee's room. "Now get on back to bed." And with that, he was gone.

One thing the experience taught Jennifer Mizicko and the rest of her family members: Death is never final, and good-bye is not forever.

"All of the amazing events surrounding my stepdad's death showed us that the dividing line between life on earth and life beyond hardly exists," she said. "We are spiritual creatures living in physical bodies. One day, each of us will shed our bodies, but our spirits will go right on living."

PART SIX

Do You Believe in Ghosts?

In spite of our best efforts at denial, mysterious encounters with otherworldly entities seem as common as ever.

Let's face it: In our culture, claiming to see ghosts is generally not taken as a positive sign. It may be good for a few laughs with friends around the campfire on a dark night deep in the woods, or at a teenage slumber party, with a flashlight pressed to your chin throwing ghoulish shadows on your face.

But that's all just for fun. If someone you know—maybe your spouse, or your sister, or a co-worker in an adjacent cubicle—suddenly starts talking seriously about seeing apparitions, you would probably back away a step or two and begin thinking about psychiatric intervention. We all know ghosts aren't real, right? Anyone who says otherwise is crazy, right?

Yet at the same time, we as a society spend millions of dollars every year on the latest spooky books and movies—the scarier, the better. What do we want from those darkly imaginative filmmakers and storytellers? Goosebumps, and lots of them. We feel disappointed if we aren't a little apprehensive about turning off the lights at bedtime. How do we expect them to deliver that? By making us believe—truly believe, even if only for a few hours—things that go bump in the night are real.

In other words, we can't make up our minds whether to scoff at the experience or seek it out.

Well, what if there is an explanation for that? For a variety of reasons—fear of ridicule, fear of nightmares, fear of attracting evil entities into our lives—we don't often let the subject of unseen spirits see the light of day. Out of sight, out of mind. But what if we are drawn to realistic and convincing ghost stories because we intuitively sense there is more to reality than our eyes normally perceive? What if we just want to know more about something we wonder about? Ghost stories offer a way to examine our feelings about that while keeping one foot on the fire escape—in case things get too uncomfortable. "That's just make-believe," we can say, and walk away.

If that describes you, then the stories in this section may push you outside your comfort zone. Why? Because the tales that follow didn't come from the pen of a playwright, novelist, or screenwriter. They often seem as improbable as fiction, but that's where the similarity ends. These experiences actually happened to ordinary people who aren't selling anything—and who are most definitely *not* crazy. They have come forward at the risk of sounding like they've come unglued to share with us events and encounters they can't explain. What's more, most of these people—and the many others we spoke to whose stories don't appear here—were firmly in the "skeptics" camp . . . before they encountered an apparition for themselves. "I never believed in ghosts and used to scoff at people who did," almost all of them said. "That is, until I saw one myself—and I *know* I saw one."

They aren't alone. Recent surveys reveal that nearly one in four

Americans claims to have encountered an apparition. Even the other 75 percent would probably relate to the spooky scene Mark Twain describes in *The Adventures of Tom Sawyer*: "Out of the stillness, little, scarcely perceptible noises began to emphasize themselves. The ticking of the clock began to bring itself into notice. Old beams began to crack mysteriously. The stairs creaked faintly. Evidently spirits were abroad."[1]

Many have experienced moments like that—walking alone on a dark night, sensing a presence in an otherwise unoccupied room, or waking suddenly to the spine-tingling feeling we are not alone. But we've been trained by our scientific worldview to ignore the messy spiritual implications and blame our overactive imagination for making things up. Researcher Brian Righi writes:

> Not that long ago, to suggest that what lurked about lonely crossroads or in dark attics was anything *other* than a ghost would have sounded ridiculous, and might have even gotten you stoned out of the village.
>
> Contrary to this, Western science finds the belief in ghosts a hard pill to swallow. After all, science measures the world around it in observable, quantifiable facts and outcomes that can be consistently reproduced, while ghosts, on the other hand, have continually given a rather poor performance under such conditions. Ghosts don't seem willing to squeeze under a microscope or into a test tube for science to dissect and examine, but to say that a lack of willingness on the part of ghosts to be examined proves they do not exist would be erroneous also.[2]

We know that a handful of stories won't answer all the questions and settle any debates. But our purpose in presenting them here is to raise a question: How did we ever come to believe that the only real things in life are those we can see, touch, taste, hear, and smell? For people of faith, the existence of an ethereal spiritual reality is not a foreign concept—it is *central* to our beliefs.

With that in mind, read on and listen to the experiences of average people who offer a glimpse into the world we can't see with our everyday eyes. Admittedly, some of the stories will raise questions for you—and maybe raise hairs on the back of your neck. In our first book, *Heaven and the Afterlife,* we discussed possible explanations for these kinds of experiences. They include overactive imaginations, disembodied spirits, and evil spirits. We make no attempt to draw firm conclusions about these accounts. But in our ongoing conversation about the afterlife, these tales represent an important and intriguing piece of the puzzle.[3]

23

The Room With a Bay Window

———— ✳ ————

As a young lawyer, Martin Herrera learned not
to discount eyewitness testimony
about things unseen.

By the time Martin Herrera was a junior in high school, he knew he wanted to become a lawyer. That's what the guidance counselor's questionnaire recommended and what his siblings predicted every time he won an argument on a technicality. He also knew he would come back home after law school at prestigious Tulane University in New Orleans to practice in the small southern town he loved. There was more money to be had in a big-city corporate law firm, but he wanted to spend his career serving the community that had given him so much.

On trips home from college, Martin often strolled the square around the county courthouse wondering which of the historic buildings he would eventually settle in with his own firm. The exercise was half-hearted, though, since he had long ago picked out his first choice: an old brick house on the corner. The yard was dominated by sprawling live oak trees draped with Spanish moss. A black wrought-iron fence lined the sidewalk in front. But for as long as he could remember, the place had been home to a music conservatory and was unlikely to be available anytime soon.

No one was more pleasantly surprised than Martin when Lydia, the elderly music teacher who owned the school, abruptly closed up shop and put the building on the market—two months before he passed his bar exam. The day she handed him the keys was one of the happiest of his life.

"I must give you one warning, however," she said to him with sudden gravity as they stood out front. "The building is haunted. That room there in particular," she pointed a thin finger at a bay window on the second floor overlooking the street.

Martin snickered to himself, sure the old woman was either crazy or playing a joke at his expense. He'd accepted years ago that the South had a long and rich tradition in both possibilities, particularly among the old-timers.

"She was pretty insistent, I must admit," he said. "But the idea of ghosts didn't fit anywhere in my Christian upbringing. Besides, I'd just spent several years and a lot of money getting a law degree that said to the world I could be trusted to be level-headed and rational. I wasn't about to start my legal career by letting it get around that I was indulging in superstitious nonsense."

Martin busied himself moving into his new building and forgot all about Lydia's spooky warning. His offices and a reception area were downstairs. The second floor held a conference room and a smaller library for filing cabinets and law books. Being a native son, it was not difficult for him to land work, and he quickly found he needed a clerk to help with the paperwork, in addition to his appointments secretary,

Helen. He hired a young woman named Rachel, who aspired to become an attorney herself one day. Her desk was in the library—right in front of a broad bay window with a view of the street.

"Rachel was perfect for the job," Martin said. "She was bright and eager and energetic. And she didn't seem to mind how tedious it was to keep track of all that paperwork. Nothing seemed to faze her."

The first sign of trouble appeared about a month after Rachel started work.

"Who was that little girl I saw this afternoon?" she asked at quitting time one day. "One of your nieces? You should introduce me."

Martin looked at her quizzically. "What girl?"

Rachel described how that afternoon she'd seen a small girl walk out of the library, across the second-floor landing, and down the stairs. She was about seven or eight years old, wearing a plain brown dress. She seemed to be headed somewhere, so Rachel didn't bother to introduce herself.

Martin and Helen wore puzzled looks as they told Rachel there had been no children in the building that day. They were sure of it.

"After an awkward moment, we all just shrugged it off," Martin said. "She admitted she'd just caught a glimpse of the girl out of her peripheral vision, so it could have been her eyes playing tricks on her. We laughed about her becoming cross-eyed or blind from looking at too many legal documents."

Always one to tease, Martin bought Rachel a pair of plastic super-vision glasses at a novelty shop and left them on her desk the next day. She took it well and said nothing more about seeing things.

But from that day on, a gradual change came over Rachel. Where she had been bright and cheerful, she began to be more quiet and withdrawn. She paid less attention to her personal appearance. And over the following weeks, the efficiency of her work slowly slipped. She became more forgetful and sometimes misplaced important documents.

"It's not like the changes took place overnight," Martin recalled.

"The best way to describe it is that she seemed increasingly depressed and withdrawn."

One day Martin felt the time had come to approach her and find out what was causing her distress. He walked up the stairs and into the library. Though it was a hot day in late summer, Martin noticed for the first time that the library was remarkably cooler than the rest of the building, where the aging air-conditioner seemed incapable of keeping up. He commented on the fact to Rachel, who was there at her desk with an open file in front of her. She agreed and said it was always cold in there.

Setting aside that mystery, Martin told Rachel his concerns about her demeanor and disposition and asked if there was anything he could do to help.

"It was as if a dam broke," he said. "She told me in a flood that she had decided to quit her job. She said she was going crazy and that she couldn't get a grip on her feelings anymore. She felt so *sad* all the time, for no apparent reason."

Martin didn't know what to say. He was not equipped to be a counselor. And since he hadn't grown up with any sisters, he'd always felt awkward in handling women's moods. But when he saw the joke glasses he'd given Rachel lying on the desk, intuition prompted him to ask if this had anything to do with the little girl she thought she saw weeks ago.

Rachel hesitated before answering. "Yes," she said at last.

There ensued a long pause, as if Rachel were debating saying more. Finally, she explained that the little girl had begun appearing to Rachel every few days and not just in fleeting glimpses, but in sustained moments as well. At random times, she would be sitting on the hallway floor beside the staircase, or standing at the window gazing out—long enough for Rachel to see her in more detail. The girl looked solid, like a living person, though with less color in her skin and clothes. She wore old-fashioned shoes and stockings, and always had on the same plain dress. Her dark hair was cut short, and she was thin to the point of looking unhealthy. Rachel had tried to speak to her or make eye contact, but the girl acted as if she were oblivious to her presence. There was sadness in her expression.

"And no, my eyes have not been playing tricks on me," she concluded. "And yes, I know it sounds crazy—and it sounds like *I'm* crazy. But those are the facts."

Martin stood there dumbfounded. "I didn't know what to say. I couldn't deny that Rachel really believed what she was telling me, but I wasn't ready to start thinking seriously about ghosts in the attic, much less right in our office. I was marshalling all the usual arguments about the power of the subconscious mind and all that Freudian stuff I'd learned in college—when I suddenly felt the hair on my neck stand up. You know, like when you're a kid and you're out walking at night and you're just *sure* somebody is right behind you? *That* feeling."

He turned to look, but no one was there. Still the feeling persisted, like there was something just outside his vision he couldn't quite discern.

"It didn't feel evil or threatening," he said, "just very unhappy. I suddenly felt inexplicably lonely."

That afternoon, Martin did two decisive things: He moved Rachel's desk downstairs into Helen's office, and he called Lydia on the phone.

"She didn't seem too surprised to hear from me," he recalled. "She repeated her claim that the building is haunted. I asked if she'd ever actually seen a ghost. She replied that *she* never did, but several of her students reported sightings over the years, mostly of a young girl. As for Lydia, she'd never been able to use that room for anything other than storage. 'There was too much bad memory in there,' she told me."

"Memories of what?" Martin asked her.

Lydia didn't know for sure, but said she always assumed it

had something to do with the orphanage that once occupied the building.

That sent Martin to the public library and the county courthouse in search of records to substantiate Lydia's improbable claim. Sure enough, the house had been built by one of the town's founders in the 1830s. In 1899, the family patriarch died and left the building to a privately owned orphanage. It served in that capacity until the early years of the Great Depression.

One news story from 1918 preserved on microfiche in the county library caught Martin's attention. It reported on the severe toll the Spanish Flu had taken that year on residents of the town. Perhaps some of the dead were children, Martin thought. Perhaps one of them had died in the room with the bay window.

"All of this was way over my head," he said later. "I'd been taught as a child by my parents that whenever you find yourself in a circumstance like that there is only one thing to do—*pray*. So I gathered some people from my church that I trusted not to laugh me out of town, and we went upstairs to the library and prayed. I felt silly at first—and I thought these people would think this lawyer had lost his marbles—but we asked God to either banish it if it was a demon or help it home if it was a human spirit that somehow got stuck here. And apparently he answered."

Rachel kept her job and since then has returned to her former self. And the room with the bay window is the hottest one in the whole building.

24

Attention-Starved Spirits

———— ✳ ————

An early nineteenth-century colonial house
in Connecticut wasn't as empty as Patrick and
Donna Harrigan assumed when they bought it.

In December 1991, Donna and Patrick Harrigan were ecstatic—and
relieved. It was the day they finalized the deal to buy a historic house
on Main Street in Newtown, Connecticut. They had spent their last
nickel to make it happen and had driven to the closing meeting in a
moving truck packed with all their worldly belongings.

It was a bold gamble, but one that symbolized the new life they
were creating together. After enduring a painful divorce, Donna was
eager to make a home with her new husband, Patrick—the *right* man for
her and a good father to her young daughter, Sarah. God was giving
her a second chance, and she wasn't about to miss it.

Newtown is steeped in early American history. Purchased from the

Pohtatuck Indians in 1705, the town was incorporated in 1711. French General Rochambeau's army encamped in the area in 1781, on their way to the fateful battle at Yorktown–and the end of the Revolutionary War. French soldiers used the weather vane atop the town hall–just a block away from the Harrigans' new home–for target practice.

Their house was built in 1810 by Matthew Curtiss Jr. as a home for his daughter. It stood right next door to his place, a classic colonial-era saltbox-style house built in 1750. The Matthew Curtiss House, as it is known today, is a museum operated by the Newtown Historical Society. Upon moving in next door, Donna and Patrick learned from society volunteers that their house actually replaced an older one that had burned to the ground.

"The house was grand, with high ceilings and a great front porch," Donna recalled. "It had a rustic stone foundation on a dirt floor in the basement. The walls down there were made of stones piled on top of each other. You could see the hand-hewn beams and floor joists throughout the basement and attic. There was a sense of the passage of time everywhere you looked."

The new family got busy settling in. During their first winter, the ancient oil stove in the basement called it quits, but that didn't dampen their enthusiasm. They heated the place with two wood-burning stoves–one on the ground floor that warmed the kitchen, breakfast area, dining room, and large living room; and one upstairs to heat the three bedrooms, bath, and landing.

All was well.

Yet almost immediately, Donna began to smell the sweet fragrance of flowers in bloom and to feel cold breezes inside the house that she couldn't account for–especially on the upstairs landing by the master bedroom. Like most rational people, at first she shrugged it off. As Patrick pointed out to her, the house was more than a hundred eighty years old, with single-pane windows and practically no insulation. The old girl could be forgiven a chilly draft or two.

But when the sensations persisted, Donna began to feel something more was going on. The cold, flowing air was more than a draft. It was a *breeze*, even when all the windows in the house were tightly closed. And the scent of flowers in the air was not just a hint of perfume—it was a powerful aroma.

One day, Donna and Patrick were standing in the kitchen talking about the oddities she'd been experiencing upstairs. Since moving in, they had learned that nearly every house on the street was rumored to be haunted, often backed up by spine-tingling stories of strange happenings. Upon hearing which house the Harrigans had purchased, locals frequently asked if they'd had contact with any ghosts yet.

"I never took that sort of thing very seriously, but with all that had been happening, it suddenly seemed more possible to me," Donna said. "One night in the kitchen, I rather sheepishly told Patrick I thought these experiences might be supernatural."

Patrick, however, was adamant: Ghosts don't exist.

"I was 100 percent skeptical," he explained. "I am a touch-it-and-see-it kind of guy. I told Donna there was no need for exotic or spooky explanations. Everything she described was the natural result of living in a drafty old house."

He said as much to his wife that night in the kitchen: "Be reasonable. Ghosts exist in the imagination and on the big screen—not in houses, even old ones."

At that moment, as if on cue from a theatrical director backstage, water suddenly poured full force from the kitchen sink faucet just a few feet from where the couple stood. *Steaming-hot* water. Patrick rushed to turn it off.

"It had certainly never done that before and never did it again," Donna said. "In fact, ordinarily you had to stand there with the water running for a couple of minutes, waiting for it to heat up. This time the water came on full blast and was piping hot all at once."

Donna just laughed at the eerie coincidence, because the thought of sharing the house with a ghost didn't frighten her. She hadn't sensed the presence of anything evil or menacing, and didn't mind the occasional benign manifestation. But Patrick was not ready to let go of his belief that everything in the world—no matter how mysterious it might appear at first glance—had a logical, rational explanation.

"He was determined to prove that it was just an old faucet that had been left on and that was forced open by some pressure build-up," Donna remembered. "He spent a long time, what seemed like hours, standing at the sink trying to make it happen again. After all that time, he was only able to get the faucet to drip with cold water."

According to Patrick, it was *three* hours—without success. "I'll admit it spooked me a little for the water to just turn itself on like that. But I still wasn't about to say there were ghosts in the house. Just because I couldn't figure it out didn't mean there wasn't a perfectly reasonable explanation."

A couple of months after the family moved in, they invited an insurance agent to come over one evening to discuss the policies his company had to offer. When the young man arrived, they decided to meet where they would not be disturbed by Sarah and the family dog, Tex, who were playing upstairs. The dining room was ideal, since it had three doors they could close for privacy. One opened inward from the entryway; the other two opened outward—to the kitchen and the living room.

"The agent's pitch took about half an hour," Patrick said. "The time had come for him to sign us up and sell us something—and he had us on the hook, by the way. We were sold."

Before getting down to business, the friendly young man casually asked—like so many others had—whether Donna and Patrick had seen any weird things in the house to make them think it was haunted. The couple looked at each other, silently trying to decide how much to share with their visitor.

"But before we could say anything, all three doors in the room flew open at the same time and smacked into the walls—*wham!*" Patrick said. "It was like a gust of wind caught them and threw them open."

Without a word, the insurance salesman quickly gathered up all the pamphlets and brochures spread out on the table, stuffed them into his satchel, and scurried from the house. He never looked back and never contacted the Harrigans again, giving up a sure sale.

"After seeing where we lived, I guess he figured we were too high-risk," Donna said with a chuckle.

Still, Patrick looked for mundane answers.

"I thought it could have been caused by a difference in temperature in the house," he explained. "Our only heat came from the woodstove on the other side of the closed doors. They weren't really latched, so maybe the air flow pushed them open. Of course, there is the fact that only one of the doors opened *into* the room. The other two swung outward. I admit I could never come up with a plausible reason for that."

One night that summer Donna woke up from a deep sleep, startled. What was that sound? She looked at the clock on her bedside table—*2:11.*

Then it happened again—a series of three perfectly rhythmic *bang*s that shook the entire house. Her heart pounding, she nudged Patrick awake. Before he was fully conscious, the three bangs repeated. Again the whole house trembled.

Patrick was wide awake now, having heard—and felt—the last round of loud percussive noises for himself. They repeated once more.

"My first thought was that someone was ramming a car into the side of the house," he said. "I was trying to get dressed and downstairs before the whole thing came down. I've never been in an earthquake, but I imagine that's what it feels like."

Patrick ran outside and around the house, frightened by what he might find. But he never expected to see—*nothing at all*. There was no car, no people, no tree fallen on the roof. He inspected the entire house, inside and out. Being summertime, the new boiler they'd installed was turned off. The hot water heater was functioning normally. There was no sign of teenagers playing a prank. And Newtown was not experiencing an earthquake.

"I stayed up the rest of the night trying to find some explanation for what Donna and I both heard and felt," Patrick recalled. "But I never did. There was no damage to the house, no physical evidence at all. To this day I have no idea what that was. It rattled me, no doubt about it."

All these years later, Patrick still describes himself as a skeptic—though, perhaps no longer 100 percent.

"It was interesting and makes for great conversation," he said. "My opinion, after all that, is that if there are ghosts, they are not going to harm you. My faith in God leads me to believe we had nothing to fear. Our experiences never really felt menacing, even when we were freaking out. That said, if the walls had started oozing blood or something like that, I'd have had the family out of there in a flash."

Donna thinks there really were ghosts present in the house, and that they were simply trying to be recognized. "Those strange occurrences nearly always happened right when we were talking about the possibility that the house was haunted," she said. "It's like they were acting out to get our attention and saying, 'Yeah, we're here!'"

The Harrigans left their house on Main Street two years later when Donna got a new job in another city. They've encountered no attention-grabbing "spirits" since then.

"Even the Bible talks about spirits," Patrick said. "So I believe it's possible for ghosts to be around. But I'll probably never know for sure if that's what caused all those odd things at our house. Something definitely happened—I just can't say what."

25

Treasure on Earth

While house-sitting for a friend's mother,
Alex and Leah Nagel apparently looked like
trespassers to the woman's dead husband.

After finishing his master's degree in economics at Texas Tech University in Lubbock, in May 1996, Alex Nagel had planned to return home to Pacific Grove, California, to work in his family's printing business while he saved money to continue his education and get a doctorate. His wife, Leah, had quit her job as a graphic designer; they had taken their son, Josh, out of preschool; and they'd given the landlady notice of their intention to move. She had already rented the place to a new tenant.

But when Alex was offered a last-minute position as an adjunct professor at the university, it was an opportunity he couldn't pass up. He would teach four undergraduate courses the following fall semester. The pay wasn't great, but it was enough. And it was a step in the direction of his ultimate ambition—to become a full professor and eventually land a tenured position somewhere.

That only left one question: What to do for the summer? It was too late for Leah to get her job back, and the employment market wasn't very encouraging at the moment. After a couple of weeks, it began to look like financial necessity might overrule opportunity, and they'd wind up in California anyway.

That's when Leah received a call from her friend Jan. She knew of the couple's predicament and claimed to have the perfect solution: Would they be interested in house-sitting—or more precisely farm-sitting—for Jan's mother, Carol, for six weeks that summer while she went on a long overdue vacation cruise with her sister? Her husband had passed away the previous year. While alive, he'd always resisted spending money on such "foolishness." Alex and Leah could live in the house free of charge, and Carol would pay them to take care of the few remaining animals on the place—an aging horse, a passel of chickens, and a few cats.

"We thought about it for, oh, about sixty seconds and then agreed," Alex said. "It sounded like an answer to prayer to us—and it would be great for Josh to be around animals for a few weeks."

It was settled, and a week later Alex and Leah arrived to take temporary possession of their new home, a two-story clapboard farm-house, about twenty miles outside the city. Carol and her husband, William, had grown mostly cotton there for nearly all their married life. Lubbock, located in the Texas panhandle on the high plains, has a geography that can be summed up in one word: flat. You can see for miles in any direction. The evening the family moved in, thunderclouds began gathering in the west and the wind kicked up.

"At first glance, the place appeared to have real country charm," Leah said. "But the closer you looked, it became obvious that it was tired and run-down. I guess that's what happens when a farmer gets old and his kids move off to an easier life somewhere else."

Even so, the house was comfortable and would be a perfectly fine place to spend part of the summer. They got acquainted with the layout and unpacked their things. Before she left, Carol had insisted they sleep in the master bedroom because the others had been taken over by storage and would be too difficult to make ready for them. Josh would sleep on a rollaway bed beside theirs. Alex thought it odd that there was a night-light plugged in to every outlet along the bedroom walls–three in all–but he just shrugged it off.

By nightfall, the line of thunderstorms that had been approaching all evening finally arrived. Rain fell in buckets, and the house groaned in the wind. Loud claps of thunder rattled the windowpanes. Alex expected Josh to be terrified, but the four-year-old giggled and squealed with every new flash and boom.

"When we were getting ready for bed, I went around the room and turned off all the night-lights," Alex recalled. "Josh had outgrown his at home, and I had trouble sleeping unless it was good and dark."

Alex was the last to get in bed. After reading for a few minutes, he turned off the lamp on the nightstand.

"As soon as that light went off," Alex said, "the hair on my head stood straight up. You know how you can sense when someone comes up behind you? I had that feeling, but times ten. And instead of being behind me, I would have sworn there was somebody right in front of my face."

Alex fumbled awkwardly with the unfamiliar lamp to turn it back on. He sat up, half expecting someone to actually be present in the room. Josh and Leah were already asleep. Alex sat there long enough to chastise himself for acting like a spooked kid again. He'd been terribly afraid of the dark as a child, but had long since gotten over that. He decided to lie down and try again.

He switched off the light and instantly felt the same presence again. And this time he knew that whatever it was didn't seem happy.

"I had that light back on real quick," he said. "I looked at the cheap plastic night-lights I'd turned off earlier and suddenly had an idea why they were there in the first place."

He got up and turned each one back on. Then he climbed back in bed and turned off the lamp—his eyes wide open. He was acutely aware of the sound of rain dripping off the roof outside and of every creak in the whole house. But this time, Alex did not feel the menacing presence as he had a few moments before.

Soon he fell asleep.

At breakfast the next morning, the sunshine through the windows looked brighter than usual. Leah said she had slept like a rock. Josh was watching cartoons on TV in the living room. By the time Alex finished his oatmeal, he was convinced the spooky incident from the night before had been no more than a weird dream. He laughed at himself and blamed it on the microwave Chinese food they'd had for dinner.

"I was getting ready to go out and play farmer and feed the animals when Josh came into the kitchen," Alex said. "I'll never forget it. He said, 'Daddy, the man by the TV said he'll be mad if you take his coins.'"

Leah looked quizzically at Josh. "You mean the man *on* the TV?"

"No!" the boy insisted. "The man *by* the TV."

Alex and Leah both headed for the living room, but it was empty. They questioned Josh further about what he had seen—a man standing beside the TV trying to get his attention away from cartoons.

What did he look like?

An old man in a blue shirt.

What did he say?

He'll be mad if you take his coins.

Did he scare you?

No. I think he's the one who is scared.

"I didn't know what to make of *that*," Alex said. "But it certainly made me think again about what had happened the night before. I was ready to start thinking we had a ghost on our hands. I was about to tell Leah my story, when I noticed she suddenly looked distracted and a little pale."

Leah, it turned out, had a story of her own. That morning she woke up early. The sun seemed especially warm and bright after last night's storm, so she decided to have coffee outside. The chickens were already scratching in the grass for bugs beside the driveway. Songbirds filled a drooping peach tree nearby. Leah sat on a rusting water tank turned upside down to enjoy the moment of peace.

"Right then I thought I saw movement near the barn door out of the corner of my eye," she said. "I looked and was startled to see a man standing there, about twenty or thirty feet away. He was looking past me at the house. I stood up and shielded my eyes from the sun to get a better look, but then he was gone. I don't mean he walked away or anything. He was just *gone*."

Initially, she concluded her eyes were playing tricks on her and dismissed the incident. But when Josh described the man by the TV, she wasn't so sure anymore. The man at the barn was old and wore a blue shirt.

Alex and Leah concluded something very strange was going on. It wasn't their imagination—at least they were pretty sure it wasn't. What to do about it was another matter. They couldn't very well pack up and leave, since they had agreed to take care of animals for another five weeks and six days. Besides, where would they go? They decided the best course of action, as always, was to ask for God's help and protection. If a little night-light could make things better, surely prayer could do a whole lot more. They spent considerable time praying throughout the house and the property, requesting that God remove any spiritual darkness and replace it with his light.

Leah said, "We also decided that if there was a ghost in the house, and if he was worried about our stealing his coins, whatever that meant, it couldn't hurt to tell him we had no such intention."

Along with Josh, Alex and Leah made a game out of playfully saying out loud in every room, "We don't want your coins."

After that, there were no more encounters with an angry spirit in the dark or an old man in a blue shirt. The family enjoyed a nice country holiday of their own until Carol returned.

They never fully solved the riddle of the experience, but months later they received another clue from Jan. She casually mentioned that her stepfather, William, had been an avid coin enthusiast. In fact, he had amassed quite a valuable collection over the years. But being perpetually worried about thieves, he hid his prize in increasingly clever places—so clever that a year after his death, Carol had still not found it.

An Eye Toward
Eternity

Visions and divine signs provide a peek into the afterlife.

Candice Tully, just shy of her fifth birthday, sat down on a park bench next to her mother, Tina, in their Fort Walton Beach, Florida, neighborhood.

"Mommy," the little girl said earnestly, "do you remember the lady and her little boy we went trick-or-treating with when we lived in Texas?"

"Yes, I sure do, sweetheart," Tina replied. "You're talking about Tricia and her son, Justin."

Candice nodded solemnly. "The mommy died in a car accident. The boy and a friend of his were also in the car, but they're okay."

Tina didn't know what to think. She hadn't heard of any tragic accident involving their old friends.

That was as far as the conversation went, since Tina couldn't figure out what her daughter meant, and Candice didn't seem upset.

The next morning, September 25, 2009, Tina received a call from a friend in Texas who informed her that Tricia had been killed in a car wreck the day before. Thankfully, the caller said, Justin and another boy riding in the vehicle survived.

Deeply shaken, Tina wasn't sure how to interpret her daughter's comment in light of the terrible news. She decided to probe gently and matter-of-factly to avoid upsetting or frightening the girl.

"Candice, how did you know this happened?" she asked. "Did you see the accident or did someone tell you about it?"

"Oh, I saw the accident, Mommy," the girl explained. "I was the only one who saw it. The crash happened with a blue truck, and the man driving had brown hair."

Tina asked her daughter how she knew the woman was dead.

Candice pointed to the toes her mother had recently broken. The girl said, "All her bones were broken, Mommy, just like the ones in your foot."

You might call them visions, divine signs, or extraordinary spiritual insights. Sometimes for brief moments, the curtain between this world and the next is pulled back to allow a fresh glimpse or new awareness.

Of course lots of people in our rational, scientifically oriented society call such experiences coincidences, flukes, or chance occurrences. To get an idea of our cultural bias against treating visions as valid and valuable clues to the nature of the afterlife, we need look no further than the dictionary. *Webster's* defines a vision as "some product of the fancy or imagination; an imaginary or unreal thing."

A few entries later we read that a *visionary*—one who has visions—is a "dreamer; an impractical schemer."

Hmm. Imaginary? Unreal? Impractical?

We doubt the apostle Paul would have used those words to describe his experience on the road to Damascus. Called Saul at the time, he was on his way to persecute and imprison followers of Jesus.

> As he neared Damascus on his journey, suddenly a light from heaven flashed around him. He fell to the ground and heard a voice say to him, "Saul, Saul, why do you persecute me?"
>
> "Who are you, Lord?" Saul asked.
>
> "I am Jesus, whom you are persecuting," he replied. "Now get up and go into the city, and you will be told what you must do."
>
> The men traveling with Saul stood there speechless; they heard the sound but did not see anyone. Saul got up from the ground, but when he opened his eyes he could see nothing.[1]

The episode—for Paul and the men with him—was as real as it gets. For three days, he was blind and refused to eat or drink anything. And the experience had vast practical implications. As a direct result, he not only ceased his efforts to stamp out nascent Christianity, but he also became its leading advocate and promoter around the Roman Empire. The effects of his vision and transformation are still being felt today.

Obviously, the experiences of a first-century saint and a twenty-first-century girl are quite different. These examples—and many more throughout the intervening centuries—show that the spiritual world sometimes interrupts our lives at times and in ways that can be dramatic, inspiring, and perhaps plain old mysterious.

The stories that follow serve to demonstrate that visions still occur today among quite ordinary people. They represent a revealing source of information in our quest to better understand the afterlife. In fact, in some cases, such visions are practically identical to near-death experiences—only without the physical trauma that brings about a brush with death. They are just as vividly real—and just as life changing. Some of the visions feature divine signs—God's way of bringing comfort during anguished times. The effects of such incidents are powerful, and most of the people we spoke with were overcome with emotion in the telling, even years later.

Read on and discover for yourself the very *modern* power of visions to illuminate what happens after death and confirm that God is still very much involved in the world.

26

"Tonight I'm Going to Take You to Heaven."

— ✳ —

Grieving the loss of his son, Trevor Yaxley
didn't have to die to go to heaven for a visit.

A few days before Christmas 1986, the residents of northern New Zealand got what they'd been praying for—an end to the punishing drought that had left the island's normally verdant landscape parched and brown.

But they didn't expect the first rain in months to arrive on the powerful and destructive winds of Cyclone Raja, which was currently making its way northward in the Pacific toward Fiji.

On the evening the storm arrived, Trevor and Jan Yaxley had just finished leading an evangelical rally for several hundred local teenagers at a meeting hall not far from their home. Darkness had fallen by the time they left the building and headed into the torrential rain and lashing wind. They were soaked the moment they stepped out the door.

Trevor pulled the car onto SH 1 for the short drive home. He hadn't gone far when a fierce gust of wind pushed the car effortlessly across the pavement into the oncoming lane. He steered back to the proper side of the road and commented to Jan how fortunate they'd been that no cars were coming toward them just then.

"It was absolutely blowing a gale," Trevor said. "Really terrible weather and very dangerous driving conditions."

As they carefully made their way through the storm, they thought of their two children who had left the rally an hour earlier and headed home along the same route. Sixteen-year-old David was driving, his sister Rebecca in the car with him. The concerned parents said a prayer—and tried not to worry about the hazardous stretch of road ahead.

The Yaxleys were quite familiar with highway accidents. As well-known Christian ministers in the area, they often accompanied emergency responders to accident scenes to provide spiritual assistance as needed. Only a week ago they'd been present when a young person died in a terrible wreck. In other words, they knew better than most people what was at stake on a night like this one.

"By the time we reached Dome Valley, just a few miles from home, we saw that the road ahead was completely blocked by an accident," Trevor said. "It was a horrendous sight, with flares burning on the road and lights flashing everywhere. A helicopter was trying to land to assist."

There were no other cars ahead of Trevor and Jan, and he pulled right up to the police barricade in the road.

"I turned to Jan and said, 'Honey, brace yourself, I think something terrible has happened.' I told her to stay in the car and I would go see."

Jan said, "It's David! It's David! I know it's David!"

Although Rebecca was also in the vehicle, their hearts told them that something awful had happened to David.

As Trevor crossed the barricade and walked into the scene, he saw immediately that the cars involved were "totally wrecked and torn apart." The rain continued to pour, drenching him to the skin, but his only thought was the growing stone-cold awareness that one of the cars belonged to David. Just then a teenage boy named Andrew, a member of David's youth group who had been traveling safely in another car, approached and fell into Trevor's arms, sobbing and unable to speak. His presence confirmed what Trevor already suspected. Pain and dread flooded his body. He raised his hands to God.

"Somehow I said to him, 'Though you slay me, yet will I trust you.'"[1] "Even at that time I felt God clearly speaking to me. 'You just watch what takes place now, and you will see what I can do in a person's life.'"

Trevor and Jan buried David on Christmas Eve 1986. To attend the funeral, they had to leave thirteen-year-old Rebecca in the intensive care unit of the hospital being treated for injuries she sustained in the crash. She eventually recovered.

And life went on. Sort of.

The couple decided to continue their work with Lifeway Ministries, the organization they founded when Trevor left a lucrative career in business to realign priorities to his family and community. The calendar was already packed with speaking engagements and evangelical rallies.

But nearly two years after David's death, the pain was still fresh for Trevor. The joy and light had still not returned to his life. Trevor and Jan had seen many thousands of people touched by God in their ministry, but Trevor's heart was still wounded and raw.

In 1988, the Yaxleys embarked on a major ministry trip to the

South Island. After twelve days of leading as many as three meetings a day, Trevor and Jan arrived in the city of Invercargill for the final rally of the tour. They were physically and emotionally exhausted. That night, waiting to begin, Trevor looked out over the packed auditorium. Every seat was filled—except for one. It was in the front row, right where David always sat when he accompanied his parents to meetings like this one.

"David was a very hip kid, very cool," Trevor recalled. "The other kids loved having him around. He was also a Christian leader. He was my chief cheerleader at these engagements. When I saw that empty seat that night, I felt his absence very strongly. Then the devil said to me, 'See, he's gone. Everything will be a shambles. Nothing will happen tonight, because you don't have anything to say.'"

It didn't work. Trevor told Satan to stand aside. And the evening was a tremendous success.

That night, Trevor fell into bed worn out, body and soul. He missed David as much as ever. He began to pray. In spite of all he could see the Lord doing through their ministry, he asked God for reassurance that he and Jan were in the right place, doing the right thing.

God answered: *"Yes, you are. And, by the way, tonight I'm going to take you to heaven."*

What was that? Trevor had learned to trust the sound of God's voice when he spoke in times like this. But had he heard correctly? Was God really promising to take him to heaven?

"Somehow I knew that didn't mean I was going to die," he said. "But I was amazed at the possibility it might really happen. I tried to go to sleep. But when God has said he's going to take you to heaven, you can't go to sleep!"

Trevor tossed and turned most of the night.

"At about six o'clock, it was still dark outside. I was lying on my back, and I said to God, 'You haven't got much time left, only a couple of hours.' As the words left my mouth, an absolutely incredible thing happened."

Suddenly Trevor felt as if he were flying upward so fast he could barely breathe. He felt pressure on his body, like the wind resistance one feels riding a motorcycle very fast—only greater. The tremendous speed he was traveling made it difficult to open his eyes. He had the impression that he was moving past many bright lights.

All at once, he felt an enormous "thump" as his feet landed on solid ground.

"At first, I felt really wobbly," he said. "As I opened my eyes, the sights and sounds and scents just flooded my senses. All of them were instantly heightened beyond anything I had ever experienced. I was especially aware of the most amazing fragrance. It is completely impossible to explain how wonderful it was. You don't just smell it. You *experience* it. It affects your whole body. It affects *you*."

Trevor immediately felt an overwhelming sense of well-being. His body was flooded with an intense feeling of acceptance, love, and understanding, like he was the only person in the world.

He looked to his left and beheld an immense, beautiful tree.

"I immediately noticed some incredible differences between this tree and the ones we have on earth," Trevor said. "It was emitting its own light. Light didn't shine on things there, it came out of everything. I was surrounded by light."

As he was trying to cope with his heightened emotions, Trevor noticed he was standing on a path that wound its way downward away from the tree. Just then he sensed there was someone standing behind him. He turned and saw a person who emitted light in the same way as the tree. Trevor didn't notice anything about him except his radiant face that exuded love and kindness—and the fact that he was speaking without moving his lips. Communication was forming in Trevor's mind without the need for sound.

"Hey, how are you doing?" the man asked, very matter-of-factly. "How long have you been here?"

"I said that I had just arrived," Trevor recalled. "But I was stunned, because it was like he was speaking with two voices. Underlying what he'd said was this stream of affirmation that continuously kept telling me what an amazing person I am and what wonderful qualities I have. I will never be able to express the joy I felt at this."

As the person was speaking these things, Trevor noticed a building nearby that looked like a child's playhouse. The man beckoned him to follow inside. He did, ducking his head to get through the low doorway. Once inside he saw a spacious room filled with equally radiant people.

"As I looked at all these people, I saw an expression come on the face of the one who had been speaking to me," he recounted. "Everybody inside looked up at me and smiled. Suddenly I just knew that everything had been prearranged. You just know, you don't have to ask. I knew God had set this up for me as a father. I knew my son was behind me. I turned around, and there he was on the path."

Just as he had often done in life, David smiled at his father and enticed him to play a game of chase. "See if you can catch me!" he called, turning and running down the path past the tree.

"My son looked so full of life!" Trevor said. "This wasn't a dream. It was utterly real."

Trevor didn't want to chase David. He wanted to *hold* him. He excused himself from the people in the playhouse and took off running. As he ran, he noticed he was not expending energy at all the way he would have on earth. He didn't grow winded or tired. He felt as if all the energy of heaven was *one*—and it was all fused into himself.

"As I was following David, I noticed I was standing on these unbelievable flowers. They were transparent, with incredible colors like you can't imagine—and they were *humming*. I know how crazy that sounds, but they were humming praise to God. Nothing was broken. I felt guilty about even standing on them, but they would just stand straight back up again."

Trevor continued running after David. The path led through a stand of trees where leaves were falling to the ground in a carpet of light. Again Trevor was struck that there was light everywhere, coming from everything. Then he caught up with David, and they embraced.

"I could feel the muscles on his back and could smell him again," Trevor said. "The look on his face was one of absolute delight and peace. His eyes were so clear, and he was so pure it was almost scary. There was nothing in him other than purity. He was changed, and yet he was still himself. He was perfect."

David said, "How is Mom's garden going? I'm glad to see you are still growing things."

Just before he died, David had helped Trevor plant a garden in the yard for Jan.

"I said it was doing great, but I didn't want to talk about Mom's garden. I asked him, 'How are *you*?'"

"Wonderful! Let me show you around."

David took his father's hand and led him through a field covered in what looked like "freshly mown velvet." Everything was arranged with a "random perfection." There were houses spread across the field that Trevor knew were waiting to be occupied by God's people. He was overcome by the beauty of what he was seeing and the joy of being with David. He began to cry.

"Don't cry, Dad," David said tenderly. "Nobody cries here."

"I'm just so happy, I can't help it!"

"But there is no *need* to cry."

As they were speaking, David's voice suddenly began to fade, and things felt to Trevor as if they were "going in reverse." He felt himself moving again—backward this time—at incredible speed. He felt his body hit the motel bed where he'd spent the night back on earth. It landed with a jolt and a thump. He immediately burst into tears, and Jan jumped out of bed and ran to his side. For a long time he only sobbed while Jan comforted him.

"I couldn't talk about my experience to anybody but Jan for a long time," Trevor said. "Everybody told me, 'You're different, what's happened?' But I couldn't tell the story. It was too close. Even so, from that day on I truly was a totally different man. My grief had gone and my joy had returned. I was able to smile and laugh and play again."

Trevor's trip to heaven that night energized his desire to tell others about God's grace and salvation—something he and Jan have continued to do through various ministry opportunities. Having seen firsthand the wondrous eternity people give up in exchange for a few years of earthly pleasure, he is determined to spend his life helping them make a different choice.

"God loves us so much and has put so much effort into what he's prepared for us," he said. "I see now that I'm living my life for future generations and for heaven as well. I want heaven to be proud of my life. That is a profound responsibility."

27

The Scars to Prove It

———— ✳ ————

After being electrocuted and pronounced dead,
Art Walters returned to life—but the
miracles didn't stop there.

On the morning of September 18, 1971, Art Walters rolled out of
bed as he usually did—straight onto his knees. Having escaped a few
years ago, with God's help, from a dead-end life of addiction to drugs
and alcohol, he knew better than anyone how easy it would be to let
temptation drag him back into the past. It had become his habit to
avoid that possibility by dedicating each day to God right from the
beginning.

He had been married for two years to Vicki, a Christian woman
who shared his dream of reaching out to street people, especially those
whose lives had also been ravaged by drugs and alcohol. Together they
had helped create *Casa de Vida* (House of Life), a Christian halfway

house in Santa Barbara, California. Its mission was to assist people who were trying to break free from the downward spiral of homelessness and addiction. As live-in counselors, Art and Vicki provided shelter, job training, and spiritual guidance to anyone who sought it.

To help make ends meet, residents often took on odd jobs around the community—landscaping, painting, or minor renovations and repairs. On that September day, Art was planning to supervise several ongoing projects. But first, on his knees in the bedroom that morning, his former lifestyle came to mind. He thought of all his old friends still partying, ruining relationships, and living only for themselves.

"I asked God to burn bridges in my life that morning," Art said. "I asked him to get rid of everything in my life that might still tempt me to turn back. I guess it really is true you have to be careful what you pray for."

Later, Art set out on his rounds under a gorgeous, sunny blue sky. His first task: Check in with Bud, a *Casa de Vida* resident who had become a Christian just two weeks earlier. That day, Bud was tackling a variety of odd jobs at a local motel being remodeled. Art learned that the manager had offered to give an almost brand-new, fifteen-foot television antenna to the halfway house—provided they would remove it from the motel roof. After a quick assessment of the job, Art and Bud decided to take her up on the deal.

Using a stepladder, the two men climbed onto a wooden trellis covering the patio alongside the building. From there they stepped onto the clay tile roof and made their way upward to the antenna. It was attached to a long pole that fitted into an even longer one anchored in the ground below. All they had to do was lift the top portion free and lower it down. Art and Bud took positions on opposite sides of the pole, got a firm grip, and lifted. According to their plan, it came free.

But the antenna on top was heavier than they imagined. Furthermore, its weight wasn't balanced—and the pole slowly began tilting to one side. The men strained with all their might to hold it upright, but they lacked the leverage to counteract the pole's growing momentum.

"I don't have it!" Bud shouted.

Art didn't either.

As if in slow motion, the antenna toppled onto a cluster of high-voltage electrical wires that had been strung too close to the building. The force of the impact broke through the wires and sent the live ends falling to the rooftop. Two cylindrical transformers on top of the utility pole exploded, showering the roof with sparks. A ball of fire traveled down the pole and engulfed Art and Bud in flames. The repulsive force of the electricity threw them both like rag dolls onto the roof tiles.

Art was instantly knocked unconscious. And his clothes were on fire.

"The last thing I remember," Art recalled, "was holding on to the pole and watching my hands start to bend over with it. Then everything went black, like I had been shoved into a dark closet."

He believes he died at that moment. "I was still awake and aware, I just couldn't see anything," he said.

Suddenly, Art felt a cool breeze on his face, as if a fan had been turned on. He looked to his left and saw something in the distance coming toward him—or maybe *he* was moving toward *it*. He had the impression of looking through binoculars and trying to focus on the image as it drew closer. Then Art saw clearly that the object was his own body. Looking down at himself, lying on the roof, charred and burning, he *knew* he was dead.

"Then I looked to my right and saw the huge chest of a man, from the neck down to the hands. I knew right then I was in the presence of the Lord. It was like he was too big for the picture frame. His chest took up the whole sky. I watched as his hands scooped up my body, held it for a few seconds, and then set me back down. I could feel his wonderful presence in those hands and in that embrace."

When Jesus put him back down, Art awoke in his body again—and he stood up. He was surprised to see that he was now off of the roof and surrounded by members of the fire department and ambulance crew. Art looked down at his horribly burned body.

Then he passed out.

———

Like Art, Bud had been thrown to the tile by the force of the high-voltage shock. His first thought upon seeing Art's unconscious body was that his friend was dead. Art's clothes were in flames, and the sparking wires dancing wildly across the rooftop occasionally made contact with Bud's torso and legs. It occurred to Bud that he would also be dead soon.

Although his new relationship with God was barely two weeks old, Bud cried out, "Jesus!" He thought it would be his last word. Instead, a surge of strength passed through his body and stood him on his feet. He patted out the flames on Art's shirt and pants. Though he had severe burns over 30 percent of his body, Bud dragged his friend across the tile to the edge of the roof and the patio covering where they had climbed up. Leaving Art there, Bud descended the ladder. At the bottom, he was trying to figure out the best way to get Art off the roof.

When he looked back up, Bud was astonished to see a man standing on the roof. He held Art's limp body in his arms and was handing him down the ladder. Bud took his friend from the man and laid him on the ground. When he looked up again, the man had vanished. He later told Art he was certain it was an angel of God, sent to help.

When emergency medical technicians arrived, they quickly pronounced Art dead. They estimated he'd been dead at least ten minutes.

He had second- and third-degree burns over 70 percent of his body—and no measurable signs of life.

Bud sat nearby and began to repeatedly pray, "Please, Jesus, don't let him die!"

At that moment, Art abruptly stood up from the stretcher as if someone had lifted him to his feet. He looked around, then at himself—and collapsed. The EMTs sprang to action. They packed Art's body in ice gathered from the motel ice machine. On the way to the hospital, Art's heart stopped beating five times. Each time he was revived.

Over the next three weeks, Art Walters had every reason to wish he had died that day. Once he regained consciousness at the hospital, he was in constant, excruciating pain. A renowned British plastic surgeon, Dr. John Chapple, "coincidentally" was on duty in the emergency room when Art was rushed in, so he received excellent care. But there was nothing anyone could do to diminish the agony of his deep and widespread burns.

The prognosis was not good. Doctors told Vicki and Art that he could die of fluid loss, infection, even exhaustion from his treatment. If he survived, he might be paralyzed or might have suffered heart or brain damage. There would certainly be severe scarring over his entire body, including his face. In fact, Dr. Chapple had already decided that damage to Art's face warranted immediate surgery.

"I heard that and visualized myself as a hideous monster for the rest of my life," Art said. "I cried out to God, 'What are you doing to me?'"

God answered Art's prayer with a promise—and a question. "*I can heal you completely. But would you be willing to carry these scars for my glory, as a testimony to what I can do?*"

Art agreed, though he didn't know exactly what that meant for his future.

God replied, *"As a sign to you, I will heal your face so there is no scarring."*

The next morning Dr. Chapple took one look at Art's face and canceled the surgery.

"He came in, looked at me, and in that British accent said, 'My, how remarkably your face has healed overnight.'"

Still, the pain went on. And the rest of his body remained in critical condition.

Every day Art underwent the horror of having his bandages changed. First, nurses stood him upright using his specially designed mechanical bed frame. Then he spent half an hour stepping away from the mattress that had stuck to the seared flesh on his back. Once free, he was taken in a wheelchair to a basement whirlpool and immersed in body-temperature water. There he endured more agony as nurses pulled away the old bandages to prepare his body for new ones.

"I screamed and screamed night and day," Art said. "I couldn't eat or drink. I couldn't sleep. It was horrible. Not knowing when the pain would end was the worst part."

Doctors expected Art to be in the hospital undergoing treatments for at least three months. After four weeks, things were not going well. Infection was a constant concern, as was keeping Art's body hydrated. He was allowed no visitors except Vicki. Even then, she was dressed in full protective clothing so that only her eyes were visible to Art. On top of everything else, he battled with growing despair.

A bright spot in his day came when a Christian nurse would snatch a few fleeting moments to read to him from Scripture. One verse in particular gripped Art's heart: "No temptation has seized you except what is common to man. And God is faithful; he will not let you be tempted beyond what you can bear. But when you are tempted, he will also provide a way out so that you can stand up under it" (1 Corinthians 10:13).

A way out. That sounded good. "I knew God was telling me to keep looking for the way out he had provided and not to give up," Art said.

Several weeks into his recovery, Art spotted greenish smoke pouring into his hospital room around the door. His first panicked thought was that the building was on fire. But he quickly realized that an evil spirit had entered the room, filling it with thick, oppressive smoke.

"It was a satanic presence," he said. "I started hearing a voice in my head saying, 'Wouldn't you like to be done with this pain? It could be over in a matter of seconds. Go on, you can do it.'"

Art's right arm had been burned from his armpit to his fingertips, but he somehow managed to reach for a pair of scissors on the bedside table. He picked them up and felt an unseen force pushing his hand toward his body.

He began to pray, "But I am a Christian! I serve God. I know this isn't right."

Still something pressed on his hand, moving it closer to his chest. He continued to pray—and then felt another force take hold of his clenched fist and push in the opposite direction. He felt it was the Holy Spirit responding to his prayers.

"I was in the middle of a spiritual battle, a tug-of-war, with my life on the line," Art said. "Then all of a sudden the room was filled with light. I looked and saw the Lord Jesus standing at the foot of my bed. He was radiant and beautiful! He smiled at me and put his hand on the end of my bed. Instantly, I fell asleep—a miracle in itself, since I had been unable to sleep for at least four weeks until then."

The next day when nurses entered the room to begin the daily ordeal of changing bandages in the whirlpool downstairs, they were astonished to find him asleep. As usual, they proceeded to stand his bed up and to free his skin from the mattress.

"This time, as I stepped away from the bed, I closed my eyes and saw the face of Jesus smiling at me, just like he had done the night before," Art remembered. "He told me, 'I am the way out.' I knew he was talking about the verse in First Corinthians. I kept my eyes closed, looking at his face. It seemed like only a few seconds."

But when he opened them again, his body was already wrapped in fresh bandages—without a trip to the whirlpool. The nurses had painlessly removed all the old covering and replaced it with new.

"From that moment on, things began to turn around. Surgeries were more effective, infection reversed course, and the pain was more manageable. Contrary to the doctor's prediction, I was able to walk out of the hospital two weeks later. I looked like Frankenstein, but I was walking."

Art's road to full recovery was still arduous and lasted many months. But he did recover. As for Bud, he overcame his injuries as well. Art and Vicki lost contact with him over the years; but they'll never forget how his remarkable faith and fervent prayer brought Art through the fire that day.

Today, not even Vicki can see a trace of scarring on Art's face. And God has used Art's remarkable story many times through the years to draw people to himself. The couple has continued in full-time service to God throughout the years—as missionaries to Central America and in various U.S. churches and ministries.

Art summed up his miraculous experiences: "I was given a gift— more time on earth to help people and serve God. Each day is an opportunity I try to use to the fullest."

28

Comfort in a Cloud

As her heart ached, Rita Hauck received reassurance from an unexpected source.

New mother Rita Hauck—exhausted yet elated as she lay in the hospital bed—cradled the precious bundle that had just been placed in her arms. She and her husband, Bob, had chosen to name their first child Erin Irene—Erin because it was a name they had always loved, and Irene to honor Rita's mother, Opal Irene Pope.

It was a sweet, tender moment for Rita, but one also tinged with longing. *Oh, I wish I could tell Mom,* she thought on that clear, sunny day in Hillsboro, Kansas, the last day of September 1971.

Rita had always enjoyed a close relationship with her mother. Opal was a godly woman who loved her family dearly and dedicated her life to being the best mother she could be. Rita dreamed of sharing the experience of motherhood with Opal. She saw what a wonderful grandmother Opal was to her brothers' children, and Rita couldn't wait to start a family of her own.

However, for the first six years of their marriage, Rita and Bob were unable to conceive. Opal, meanwhile, dealt with her own crisis. She developed sarcoma, cancer of the connective tissues, and doctors were forced to amputate her right leg. Despite the amputation, Opal spent more than six years fighting the cancer in other parts of her body.

For Rita, it was heartbreaking to watch her mother decline and suffer. She wasn't ready to say good-bye. She and the rest of her family prayed for a miracle, yet Opal's condition continued to worsen. Finally, at the end of summer 1970, Opal was admitted to a hospital in Enid, Oklahoma. The end was near.

Rita, a music professor at Hillsboro's Tabor College, rearranged her teaching schedule so she could support her father and be with her mother six days a week. Every Tuesday night, after a full day of teaching, she jumped into the car for the three-and-a-half-hour drive to Enid. As the fall season deepened, Rita watched leaves in the trees alongside the road change from green to vibrant reds, yellows, and browns. She enjoyed their beauty, but knew it was temporary. Winter was on its way, and the leaves would soon be gone. It reminded Rita that this time with her mother was still beautiful, but that this season would also end all too soon.

The pain Rita felt over the possibility of losing her mother and never sharing her own children with her was almost unbearable. One day as she sat by Opal's hospital bed, she tried putting it into words:

"Mother, I so long to tell you that I'm pregnant," Rita said, her eyes welling with tears. "I wish you could live to know our children. I've seen the impact you've had as a godly grandmother. You could pray over our child."

"Rita," Opal said gently, tears forming in her own eyes, "I know that God is going to give you a wonderful family someday. I don't know how it's going to happen, but I know he's going to. It's enough for me to know that my daughters have married wonderful Christian men."

On another night, when Opal couldn't sleep and Rita massaged her mother's back, Rita admitted how devastated she was by the idea of losing her. "I don't know if I can go on without you," she said.

Opal smiled. "My precious girl, all you have to do is think about what I would say or what advice I would give, and you'll know what to do."

Rita laughed. She knew it was true. Her mother was so open about her beliefs on parenting, how to love a husband, how to serve God, and so much more that Rita felt she would always understand her feelings about any topic.

Opal continued to decline. In the last days of November, doctors said she might have only three weeks left. On November 30, at the hospital, Rita's dad said to her and her sister, Connie, "We've been praying that Mother would be home for Christmas. Well, the Lord has just spoken to me. He said, 'She's going to be home.'" Then their father burst into tears.

Opal went home to the Lord the next afternoon.

——————————

Over the following weeks and months, Rita wrestled with heart-breaking grief. Though she trusted God's love and sovereignty and had moments of peace, waves of sadness continued to overwhelm her. At Christmastime, Rita again joined in the family tradition of gathering around the piano and organ at her parents' house to sing Christmas carols. Yet even as she sang, tears flowed down Rita's face. Her beloved mother would never again be part of this usually joyful scene.

In early February, Rita and Bob decided to drive to Los Angeles to attend graduation ceremonies at USC, where Bob had earned a doctorate in musical arts. It was a bittersweet time. Just two weeks before, they'd learned of a miracle: At long last Rita was pregnant. She'd conceived in the same month that Opal died. Equally amazing, Connie was also pregnant for the first time—with the same due date as Rita's.

Rita was thrilled, yet in some ways the incredible timing intensified her grief over her mother.

On the trip west, after a lunch stop in Albuquerque, Rita was behind the wheel of their white Chevy Bel Air as Bob slept in the backseat. The miles rolled past as they traveled through New Mexico's red hills on Route 66. A light dusting of snow covered the desert on both sides of the highway. The skies were mostly blue and sunny, though a cloud bank stretched across the horizon and a group of puffy clouds loomed closer.

Rita didn't pay much attention to the weather as she drove, however. Instead, she cried and prayed.

Lord, I'm asking you to help me. I don't want to be constantly grieving. I don't want to be constantly feeling the pain of Mother's death. Please give me a way to have victory in this.

Rita wiped her eyes and glanced upward. To her astonishment, the cloud directly ahead had formed the shape of the upper half of an angel, complete with a face, arms, and wings.

Time seemed frozen. Rita stared at the cloud, though whether it was for seconds or ten minutes, she didn't know.

Suddenly, Rita gasped. She recognized the angel's face.

It was her mother.

The angel in the cloud looked directly at Rita in the car. Her expression was one of sorrow.

Oh, she's sad because I'm weeping, Rita thought.

Then the angel spoke in what to Rita seemed an audible voice, though she appeared to be addressing someone else: "I wish there was some way I could communicate to my family how wonderful everything is for me here. Then they wouldn't grieve for me so much."

Out of shock and gratitude, Rita began to sob. She knew that her mother wasn't literally an angel, but she believed that this was a gift from the Lord to show her that her mom was in heaven.

The next sound to reach Rita's ears was the singing of a heavenly choir. They sang a beautiful tune she'd never heard before. The words were "Holy, Holy, Holy. Holy is the Lord God of Hosts. Heaven and earth are full of His glory."

Even as she drove and wept, Rita continued to focus on the angel cloud in the image of her mother. As she watched, the angel's arms lifted up. At the same time, two new clouds in the shape of mighty arms reached down, connected with the angel's arms, and lifted them into the bank of clouds above until no more shapes were visible.

Overcome, Rita pulled to the side of the road and stopped. She put her arms and head onto the steering wheel and let the tears flow.

Bob awoke and climbed into the front seat. He didn't say a word, but simply put his arms around Rita and waited.

Eventually, Rita collected herself enough to speak. "I've had a vision of Mother," she said. Then she smiled. She realized all her sorrow, pain, and grief were gone. Rita knew her mother was happy and whole, that she wasn't sad about the separation from her family. Indescribable relief and comfort swept over her.

Suddenly, thanks to God's love and the appearance of an angel in the clouds, Rita was at peace.

The months passed, with Rita becoming more and more excited about her soon-to-expand family. After Erin Irene was born, Rita looked out her hospital room window at the colorful changing leaves. It reminded her of the drives to Enid a year earlier and the beauty of her mother's soul and spirit, now in heaven.

She so wished she could let her mother know about Erin. Then she felt the Lord's spirit speak to her: "She already knows all about your baby. I told her. We are rejoicing together with you in heaven."

Ten days later, Connie's daughter was born. Her name was Melyna Irene. Connie and her husband hadn't yet heard Rita and Bob's choice of a middle name for Erin. Both daughters chose to honor their mother in the same way.

Three more children joined Rita's family in the following years. The family went through the usual heartaches and struggles. Yet when Rita wished for her mother's presence and advice, she realized Opal had been right—she always knew just what her mother would say.

Rita and her family experienced many joyous events as well: birthdays, high school and college graduations, weddings, and the birth of grandchildren. For Rita, each one brought back fond memories of her mother and of the angel in the clouds.

"How grateful I am for the vision God gave me that day," Rita reflected, years after the event. "It has been a healing balm, a close presence that has supported me, cheered me on, and encouraged me through the trials of life."

She continued: "I know that some people would doubt what I saw. They would probably say that if you look at a cloud's changing form long enough, you can see whatever you want to see. That doesn't matter to me—I am absolutely certain about what I witnessed. It is a testimony of God's creativity and grace. When I think about how he heard and answered my cries to him, I feel totally loved. I understand his kindness and mercy. He has blessed me over and over."

29

Eternally Anonymous

In a few short moments, David Rutherford saw enough of the nature of hell to last a lifetime.

David Rutherford could not afford to be sick—literally.

In the fall of his sophomore year at Ozark Christian College in Joplin, Missouri, David would have been an ideal poster boy for every flat-broke college student in the country. An expensive visit to the doctor's office was no more within his budget than a week's vacation in Monte Carlo.

Not only that, he couldn't afford the *time* it took to be sick. He had papers to write and tests to study for. He had ministry duties at the tiny farm-country church in nearby Alba, where he volunteered. Spending time with Suanne—who had recently become his fiancée—was definitely nonnegotiable. To top it all off, David was a member of the college basketball team—presently at the height of the season. Practice, travel, and games allowed no time to think, much less take a day off.

Nevertheless, David *was* sick and had been for weeks. What started as a simple cold had grown progressively worse. He had survived on willpower and perpetual motion for weeks. But when he developed pleurisy—a painful inflammation of the lining around his lungs—something had to give.

"It felt like having a broken rib," David said. "Every time I moved, I felt a sharp pain in my chest. I couldn't get a deep breath. Playing basketball like that was no fun. I didn't know where to turn."

Fortunately, the answer was nearer than he thought, and it had a name: Bonnie Oney. Bonnie, in her seventies at the time, was the organ player and general pillar of the church in Alba, where David ministered. She was far more than a member of the congregation to him; Bonnie was his best friend, mentor, and surrogate grandmother. She was aware of his declining health and wasn't about to stand by while he ran himself *all* the way into the ground.

"Somebody once told me there is a Bonnie in every church in America," David said. "I don't know for sure, but I have my doubts. She was such a dear saint of a woman. I have to think she was one of a kind."

Bonnie arranged for David to be seen by a local doctor, a Christian man who routinely provided care to people in exchange for whatever they could afford to pay. In his fifties, he spent a month out of every year on mission trips abroad, treating people with limited regular access to medical care.

The day David went to the clinic, the low-level fever he'd been living with for days had begun to climb. He felt exceptionally drained and lethargic. It seemed his appointment had come at an opportune time. Suanne accompanied him into the waiting area. Moments later, he left her there to follow a nurse to an examining room.

Right away, the gray-bearded doctor bustled into the room and confirmed the diagnosis: David had pleurisy. But there was no need to worry, he said reassuringly. A shot of medicine—along with a little rest—would quickly have David back on his feet.

"I would have done anything at that point to get better," David said. "I did as he said and dropped my drawers. Then I felt the needle going into my hip."

David can't say what happened next—because he doesn't remember.

He must have passed out and collapsed to the floor, since that's where he woke up moments later.

He can't recall falling or hitting the hard tile.

Perhaps the doctor was startled when David collapsed.

Maybe he opened the door and called for help from his nurses.

When they arrived, the doctor may have instructed them to help revive the stricken young man. One on each side of him, they bent down to roll him over and try to sit him up.

The doctor must have left the room.

David will never know for sure.

He was only out a few moments. His first memory after waking is of hearing a blood-curdling scream—only to realize it was coming from his own mouth. Thrashing about in terror, his fingernails were dug into the arms of the two women trying to revive him and calm him down. He heard their voices reassuring him, telling him everything was okay.

Slowly, David remembered where he was and began to settle down.

"The nurses didn't seem concerned at all, like this kind of reaction happened all the time," David said. "They said it was nothing. I wanted to scream at them, 'Nothing? You just missed *everything*. The whole world just changed.'"

What David *does* remember, once the needle entered his skin, is finding himself in a white, featureless room. It was blindingly bright. There was no discernable beginning to the room, and no end. Even so, David had the impression he was standing in a corridor of some kind— or more precisely, at the intersection of two corridors—that stretched away from him farther than he could see.

"I didn't feel any pain, or fear, or anything at first," David said. "Mostly, I was curious about that place and about what would happen next."

Suddenly, something appeared in the distance down one of the corridors. It approached David slowly, and, as it drew nearer, he could see that it was a human face—only a face, with no body. Then another appeared at the end of the second corridor. It too moved toward David. Soon, others began to follow them in a kind of parade with two processions crossing where he stood. The faces looked like they belonged to ordinary people, though he didn't recognize any of them.

"Some were male and some female. They didn't look dead, but none of them smiled or showed any emotion," David said. "I remember thinking, *Good, now I can talk to someone and get to the bottom of this. I can find out where I am and what's going on.*"

He attempted to stop one of the faces to get some answers, but he received no response. He tried again and again, but none of the faces would even look his way, much less stop and listen to him. Now they were coming faster and faster, from both directions, until they became a blur. Hundreds of dull, blank faces poured past him, each seemingly oblivious to his existence. The more the faces raced indifferently past him, the more desperate he felt for some recognition, some connection or reassurance that he was not alone. Horrible panic rose within him.

"I know that doesn't sound so bad now," David said, "but it was the most agonizing experience of my life. I felt incredibly isolated and alone, like there was not the slightest chance of belonging or ever being cared for again. It was absolutely excruciating."

David woke up on the floor of the doctor's office, a long, loud wail coming from deep within himself. He was drenched in sweat and screaming for somebody–anybody–to acknowledge or recognize him. His heart pounded wildly in his chest. Gradually he became aware of his surroundings–the examining table where he'd leaned to steady himself for the shot, the cabinet with glass doors that held medical supplies, two young nurses bending over him to help him to his feet.

His immediate sense of terror began to subside, but not the memory of that terrible loneliness. He felt it in his whole body. Embarrassed by the episode, he buttoned his trousers, joined Suanne in the lobby, and quickly left.

David struggled over the next few days to understand why his experience had been so terrifying. Slowly, he realized that God had given him a vision–a miniscule snapshot–of what hell is really like. He now knows firsthand that it is a place of absolute and complete loneliness, a desperate isolation that no one ever experiences here on earth, no matter how alone they think they are. David didn't just feel separated from God–a state many people might associate with being in hell. He was cut off from *everyone and everything* familiar and comforting. Of the hundreds of faces racing past him, not one offered him the slightest morsel of connection or contact.

"A lot of people joke about preferring to go to hell because that's where all their friends will be, or that's where the party is," David said. "What I saw made me realize it isn't like that at all. No matter where you go on earth, you have something in common with people. Even without knowing the language, it is possible to connect and communicate on a basic level. Not in hell. And it is a horrible, horrible feeling."

David went on to become a full-time pastor and now leads a dynamic church in Fresno, California. From that day on, his ministry was shaped by an extraordinary empathy with people who feel alone in the world. He considers his experience to be a gift from God, not a punishment.

"Because of the snapshot I was shown, I know that the search for connection to each other drives people far more than theology," he said. "We want to belong and be seen for who we really are. In heaven we will feel complete acceptance, and we'll know each other in full and be known. But not in hell. There will be no comfort there, not even in the company of others who share your fate. That's why my whole life mission boils down to helping people avoid hell and instead spend eternity in heaven."

30

A Helping Hand

—— ✳ ——

For Yvonne Clark, a premature labor seemed
headed toward tragedy until a surprising
vision changed everything.

Yvonne Clark smiled as she stood at the kitchen sink in her one-bedroom Seattle home. Though her hands kept washing dishes, her mind was elsewhere. She looked down at her protruding belly and wondered again at the miracle of birth. Would she have a boy or a girl? What would her baby be like? She was twenty-two years old, excited, and full of questions.

It was April 25, 1975. Yvonne's baby was due in three months. Yvonne and her husband didn't have much in the way of possessions, so earlier in the day she and her mother-in-law had shopped for a TV set. A couple of times, Yvonne had stopped to bend over after a strange and sudden pain. But the discomfort had subsided, and now she was in the kitchen with her husband and in-laws.

Yvonne turned her attention back to the dishes. It was time to think about getting something for dinner.

That was the moment when her world turned upside down.

"Oh no!" Yvonne called out. She turned to face everyone. "My water just broke!"

Everyone stared at each other, too shocked to speak. Yvonne began to cry. She realized it was much too soon. Her precious baby was suddenly in big trouble.

The family moved into action, speeding Yvonne to the hospital. She was given a room with another woman who was due in a month and at the hospital for a test. Concerned nurses and doctors hovered and hurried around Yvonne, creating such a stir that her roommate panicked and also went into labor.

At first, the hospital staff hoped they could delay Yvonne's labor, but the lack of fluid and Yvonne's body determined otherwise. She was in labor, and there was nothing anyone could do to change it.

Anxious hours passed. Yvonne was told she shouldn't bear down because her baby was too fragile and tiny. She wasn't given pain medication for fear it would be too much for the baby.

At first, the pain and contractions were manageable. But as ten hours stretched into twenty, and then thirty, Yvonne's pain, exhaustion, and fear multiplied and converged like a pack of hungry wolves. She felt tortured by questions she couldn't answer. Would she be able to deliver her baby? Would the baby live?

Finally, a dejected nurse turned to Yvonne. "I'm sorry," she said. "The baby's not going to make it. It's going to be a dry birth. It's just too early."

Yvonne became hysterical. "No, that can't be true!" she cried, tears streaming down her cheeks. "My God, why am I going through all this if my baby's going to die?"

Despondent, she turned her head away from the medical staff to look out the window. The scene did not match her mood—it was a beautiful, sunny morning. Yvonne could see another structure, probably an office building, through the glass.

And then, suddenly, there was something else. It wasn't close to the window or near the other building. It was somewhere in between, and it was huge.

Impossibly, it was a giant hand.

The open hand faced Yvonne and moved gently forward and back, the universal gesture to slow down, to be calm.

At the same time, Yvonne sensed a soothing voice speaking to her. *Everything's going to be all right,* she heard.

Somehow, Yvonne understood the voice and hand belonged to God.

Amazed, she stopped crying and turned back to the nurses. "The baby's going to be fine," she said. "It's not going to die."

The nurses didn't know what to make of Yvonne's sudden change of attitude. They had trouble finding a heartbeat for the baby and remained pessimistic. But a doctor decided to allow Yvonne's labor to continue.

Then they heard a hiccup. The baby was still alive.

Nurses wheeled Yvonne into another room. A doctor came in with forceps. Everything moved quickly. The doctor used the instrument as Yvonne fought the urge to push.

Soon a tiny, wonderful cry reached Yvonne's ears. It reminded her of the mew of a kitten. It was her new daughter.

Yvonne had little time to enjoy the moment. Her baby was whisked away for urgent medical attention. Yvonne, exhausted after thirty-six hours of labor, passed out.

Hours later, she was rolled in a wheelchair to the preemie ward, where she saw her baby. The tiny infant was like a Barbie doll, less than two pounds twelve ounces and under a foot long. Because she was premature, she was covered with body hair. She looked like a small monkey.

"That's my baby?" she asked, her voice a mixture of fatigue and joy. To Yvonne, she was beautiful.

Only later did Yvonne reflect on what she'd seen outside her hospital room window. She'd been so close to despair, to believing the word of the nurses about her baby and giving up. Only when God intervened to calm her spirit did she find the strength and hope to keep trying.

"It was incredible," she says, "just incredible."

A non-practicing Catholic at the time, Yvonne says her experience at the hospital did not immediately recharge her faith. But God was still reaching out to her. Two years ago, a co-worker invited her to a church service. When the speaker spoke of the need to be committed to God, Yvonne responded.

While on her knees at the front of the church, as the speaker prayed specifically for Yvonne, she felt a nudge on her forehead. Along with the nudge came a sense of incredible power.

It wasn't the speaker or any other person. Once again, after so many years, Yvonne felt touched by the presence of God.

Today, Yvonne works as a paralegal in San Diego. Her faith in God is stronger than ever. Her spiritual beliefs, she says, are the foundation of her life.

The premature baby who wasn't expected to live is now a newlywed and an executive for an artificial intelligence firm in Texas. Yvonne's miracle baby—Christine—is also "smart, beautiful, an amazing young woman," says her mother.

Yvonne still marvels at the birth of her daughter and God's surprising appearance all those years ago.

"Some people might say that I hallucinated and imagined the comforting hand out the window," Yvonne said. "But I know what I saw. It was God's hand, and it assured and comforted me. I'll never forget it. I cannot deny that there's a God. I've felt him, seen him, and heard him."

Further Glimpses
of the Afterlife

When we began researching this book and put out a call for unique spiritual encounters, we were surprised—stunned, really—to receive an avalanche of stories. More evidence, if we needed any more, that God continues to work in the world today as much as ever.

Since we couldn't, unfortunately, include all of the experiences, we would at least like to present several more in brief, providing further glimpses into the world beyond this one.

"Is That What Death Is Like?"

Before working in the labor and delivery unit, I spent nine years in emergency-room work. On my shift one night in the ER, a man was checking himself in for chest pain when he collapsed in the lobby at the front desk. We got him on a gurney and rushed him into the Code Blue room. We had begun CPR because he was without a pulse or respirations. The EKG monitor showed a flat line.

After no response with the appropriate IV medications, we shocked him twice. He regained consciousness and looked up at us, saying, "Wow, I was over there, and now I'm here again. That was easy. Is that what death is like?"

But before he could say anything else, his heart stopped again and he went unconscious. We shocked him again. His heart rhythm returned, and again he looked up at us, this time smiling.

"Hey, it happened again!" he said. "I was over there, and now I'm here again—just like that. Wow! Was I dead? I think I was dead. It was so easy."

Well, he did it again. His heart stopped, and immediately we shocked him. This time it took several shocks. When he finally came back, his rhythm was unstable, and the physician said we had to calm him down or we would lose him again. So we gave him morphine, and he became fairly incoherent. By that time the internal medicine doctor had joined us, and we shipped the patient off to the ICU. That was the last I heard of him.

That man had at least three round trips between this life and the next in the span fifteen minutes!

—David Hatton, pastor and nurse, Sacramento, California

Thicker Than Blood

When my dad, Rick, died in 2009 of heart disease, I took it really hard. Frankly, I was devastated, since he was a good friend as well as a great father. But an experience in his final moments gave me tremendous comfort.

For decades, Dad enjoyed close friendships with two of his high school classmates, Drayton and Lance (I always knew them as Uncle D and Uncle L). These teenagers—who grew to be men and fathers—were actually more than close friends; they were kindred spirits and soul mates. They always said, "We aren't related by blood—it's something stronger that holds us together." Amazingly, when Uncle L got drafted into the Vietnam War, Dad and Uncle D enlisted, and they were in combat together. Years later, my dad explained matter-of-factly, "We couldn't let one of our comrades go into battle by himself, now, could we?"

Each year, these three took off for a weeklong adventure together: camping in Montana, fly-fishing in Alaska, surfing in Hawaii. They even took a cross-country RV trip together (and somehow remained friends!). And they supported each other through lots of hard times as well, such as when Uncle L's wife up and left him, when Dad went broke after a failed business venture, and when Uncle D nearly died in a work accident.

Over the years, one by one they each drifted back to the spiritual faith they'd left behind in their twenties. Uncle D was raised Catholic and later in life rejoined the church. Uncle L returned to his roots as a devout United Methodist. Dad was the lone holdout for many years, but Uncle D and Uncle L finally wore him down, and Dad became serious about his faith in God during the last decade of his life.

And one by one, they started dying off. Uncle D, who had diabetes for years, passed away in 2004. He was followed three years later by Uncle L—a massive stroke took him in an instant. My dad was never the same after those losses.

A few years later, when it was Dad's turn to face the end, he lay in the ICU ward at University Hospital in Denver. He'd been there for several days, and my sister, Kim, and I stayed by him constantly (our mother had left the picture long ago). Unconscious and laboring to breathe, Dad was ready to go on. The hours lingered as Kim and I sat by the bedside, feeling completely helpless and distraught.

Early one morning, Dad suddenly sat straight up, looked toward the ceiling, and called out as clear as day, "There they are! It's my brothers. They're waiting for me." He sunk back into his pillows, lapsed into unconsciousness again, and an hour later breathed his last.

I know some people will say that's just what Dad *wanted* to see as he was slipping toward death. I don't believe it for a minute. These three men had such a strong bond that I have no doubt the others were there to welcome Dad as he arrived in heaven.

—Cassandra Holland, Denver, Colorado

Security With a Sword

After relocating to a new city for a job, I bought a house in a quaint neighborhood next to a large city park filled with beautiful old trees. What I didn't realize was that the neighborhood was overrun with drug traffickers. In fact, a dealer lived in the house next door, and his customers frequented the neighborhood at all hours of the night.

I called an alarm company to check the cost for a monitored security system. As I considered making the $35-a-month commitment, the thought occurred to me, "For that price, I could sponsor a third-world child through Compassion International!"

Suddenly a second thought occurred to me, this one even stronger than the first. I felt God saying, "Mayme, if you sponsor that child, I'll be your security system." I sponsored Stephen Henrique, a beautiful little boy from Colombia. Then I went about my business, living life in my new home and trusting God to be my protection.

My job required working long hours and I often got home after dark, too late to walk safely in the park that was a stone's throw from my house. The park was a popular place for drug dealers and users, and police had been trying to clean up the illicit activity. But it was still no place for a woman walking alone after hours.

Nevertheless, determined not to live in fear—and remembering that I had the best "security system" of all—I often laced up my tennis shoes and hit the sidewalks that meandered through the tree-lined park.

One night as I was walking, a patrol car pulled up next to me. A police officer rolled down his window and asked, "Have you seen any suspicious characters in the area?"

My heart sped up. "No, officer, I haven't seen anyone."

"Let us know if you see anything," he said. "We've gotten several calls from people who report seeing a seven-foot-tall man walking around the park, wearing a white muscle shirt, and carrying a sword."

No joke! That's exactly what he said.

I assured him I'd call if I saw anyone fitting that description. As the patrol car drove away, something struck me, and I couldn't help but laugh out loud with delight and gratitude.

I'm sure the officer had just described my guardian angel.

—Mayme Shroyer, Colorado Springs, Colorado

Ready for the Family Reunion

I was pastor at the Lebanon Wesleyan Church in Lebanon, Indiana, from July 1978 to August 1995. While there, I became well acquainted with a man named Fred Welch who in the 1950s lived in Barberton, Ohio, and worked for the Salvation Army.

Fred was married, had two sons, and his wife was six months pregnant with their third child. While working one night at the Salvation Army, he was given a message that his house was on fire. He rushed home to find it completely engulfed in flames. His entire family was lost in the blaze.

Fred had a nervous breakdown. He spent six months in an institution and nearly died. When he was released, he somehow made his way to Lebanon and found work there. He became a part of our church, experienced a changed life, and became a great encouragement to those around him.

At one point, Fred had a heart attack and had open-heart surgery at Methodist Hospital in Indianapolis. While on the table during surgery, his heart stopped, and he was without vital signs for five minutes. Later he told me the following:

"I left my body and floated toward the ceiling. I looked down on all they were doing to me on the table. I then was drawn to a strange light through what seemed to be a tunnel. When I came out of the tunnel, the great light was still there, but it was in the background. I stood on what seemed like a river, the water clear like glass and just as smooth.

"On the other side of the river were my wife and two sons. She was waving her hand for me to come across and asking me to join them. There was a marvelous feeling of peace and I wanted to go to them, but I could not cross. I suddenly was back in the operating room looking down on my body again. I saw them use the paddles to shock my heart, and the next thing I knew I was waking up in recovery with nurses and doctors all around me."

I heard Fred tell this story many times and it never changed. He was certain that his family was with God and that he was going to rejoin them again someday.

–Rev. Paul Trent, Chesterfield, Indiana

"You've Brought So Many With You!"

The devastating disease attacked Judy's body at an early age. Diagnosed with cancer at age thirty-two, this young mother lived six years beyond the initial discovery of the cancerous cells.

Three ladies from Judy's church met with her each Thursday for prayer, Scripture reading, and encouragement. They performed this act of love for more than three years, even traveling to other states when she was in medical treatment facilities.

After an extended remission period, the cancer cells resumed the process of destroying her body. In January 1996, Judy had weakened to the point that she needed continuous hospital care. She was admitted to Madigan Army Medical Center in Fort Lewis, Washington. Judy's husband was a physician on the staff at the hospital. At the time I was a U.S. Army chaplain assigned as the director of pastoral care at Madigan. I knew Judy through previous times she had been a patient there.

It was evident to all that Judy was dying. That is, all except her mother, who desperately wanted Judy to keep fighting the disease. Judy's brother had died a few years earlier, and it was a tremendous burden on her mother to have a second child nearing death.

The last night of Judy's time on earth was one of great pain. Her parents were in the room with Judy throughout the night. Her husband was at home with their two beautiful girls, who were eight and ten years old. During the early morning hours, as Judy was in such intense pain, her mother told her it was all right for her to pass on.

At about 7:00 A.M., Judy called her husband at their home. She said to him, "I am going home today." He asked what she meant. Judy said, "I am dying today."

Quickly her husband dressed the girls and made the short trip to the hospital. I remember that when he arrived he spruced up the room. Things were in disarray from the difficult night. He turned on softly playing worship music. Then he gently placed the girls, one on each side of their mother, in the hospital bed. By this time Judy's strength was so limited that she could only barely touch them.

After a few minutes, the children were removed from the bed, and we waited. In less than half an hour, we could tell the end was near.

Suddenly Judy mustered all her strength and raised up on her elbows. She looked toward the walls of the room. She was not looking at any of us. While still propped up, she whispered, "Oh, you've brought so many with you!" Joy and amazement were in her voice.

She settled back on the bed, and within minutes her breathing stopped.

Normally a person's body would be removed from the room rather quickly. But not Judy's. She had many friends, and they began coming to the hospital to be with her family. For the next six hours, the visitors were constant. There were three separate spontaneous celebration worship services held in her room. Two were led by pastors who knew her and one by a friend who was part of her prayer group. Songs, prayers, tears, and laughter mingled throughout those hours.

I can't say for certain what Judy saw in her final moments, but her words "You've brought so many with you!" are still clear and vibrant to me. I have a strong inkling she was ushered home by a welcoming throng.

—Lou Shirey, Centerville, Georgia

Strong Enough to Go Home

I had the privilege of being with C. L. Cummings, a great spiritual leader from Kansas, just minutes before his passing. He had been in the hospital and was then put in an extended-care center because his wife, Grace, was not able to care for him at home.

I was there visiting with both of them when C. L. suddenly stopped talking and began to stare at the corner of the room. Then he got up, put on his coat and hat, and said, "It's time to go." When asked where he was going he said, "Heaven. The angels are here to get me. Don't you see them?"

His wife convinced him to take off his coat and sit down. He did, only to repeat this again.

While I was there, his doctor came in and said, "Well, C. L., it looks like you are strong enough to go on home. I'll sign the papers, and you will be on your way this afternoon."

So I prayed with them and left. When I arrived at my next destination, about a fifteen-minute trip, I had a call telling me C. L. had passed away. He knew where he was going, and he was ready to go.

—Max Colaw, Bartlesville, Oklahoma

Angels on Guard Duty

Our family lived in Minnesota during our growing-up years. In 1946, I was ten and my brother was eight, and on one particular Sunday we were both sick with either the measles or the mumps. Our mother was needed to play the piano at church. She never left us home alone, so it must have been very important for her to be in church on that specific Sunday. She told us to stay in the bedroom and play checkers or other games.

There were two windows in the bedroom, each in different walls. As we were playing games, I looked up and suddenly saw a white being with wings walk past the window. It appeared to be an angel! It passed by the one window and then the other.

"Joe, do you see that?" I called to my brother.

He looked around. "What?"

I said, "There's an angel walking past the window."

Then it went by the other window again as if it were circling the house. We were in awe. I saw another angel following after the first. We were not frightened, but instead felt completely peaceful.

When our mother got home from church we were very excited, and we told her about it. She said, "How wonderful! I asked Jesus to send his angels to walk around the house to protect you while we were away."

We all were on cloud nine the rest of the day, knowing that God in heaven was watching out for us.

—Anna Rowell Jackson, Tucson, Arizona

Speaking With the Saints

As a student at Princeton Theological Seminary, I chose near-death experiences as a topic of study for my educational psychology course. Upon graduation and ordination, in my first pastorate in Dallas, Texas, my hard work as a student was blessed by a whopper of an account:

Bob was one of those highly motivated Bible students you both appreciate and want to avoid at the same time. He had several mail-order degrees from magazine-ad Bible colleges, none I had ever heard of—which means he was in my office twice a week to challenge me on the finer points of Scripture and doctrine. He was a devout, well-informed follower of Jesus.

Bob entered the hospital with a massive stroke and was there for months. Elders and I prayed over him, anointed him with oil, and waited. He was moved to intensive care and we awaited the phone call telling us he had gone to be with God. The phone call came, but it wasn't what we expected.

His wife pleaded with me, "Please come! Bob woke up, and I think he's been to hell. All he kept saying was, 'I don't want to go back! I don't want to go back!'"

I hurried to the hospital, knowing he'd likely had an NDE. When I walked into the room, Bob looked relieved to see me. I sat down and asked him to tell the whole story.

"I went there!" he said. "I was in heaven! Pastor, it's all just like the Bible says. Everything was gold: the streets were gold, the buildings, the statues, everything. Oh, pastor, you're going to love it. The gold there was so pure you could see through it. I wanted to see Jesus, and I could tell where he was. I went to him, but there were huge golden doors with no handles on them. So I started knocking and praying and asking to be let in. A man came up to me and asked what I was doing. I said, 'Jesus is in there, and I want to be with him.' He said, 'You can't. Jesus needs to be alone sometimes.' I didn't like that, so I said, 'Well, who are you?' He answered, 'Paul.' And I said, 'Paul who?' He responded, 'PAUL!' And I felt so embarrassed. But then others were there: Philip and Bartholomew and others. It was so wonderful being with them and you could ask them anything and they'd tell you."

I interrupted Bob to ask what they talked about and for how long. He said a long time, but he could remember nothing of the discussion.

Bob continued: "I finally got to see Jesus and, Pastor, it was so wonderful! It is what we're made for—I was on my face before him and everything was complete and perfect. Just to be there praising him was the completion of my soul. But after a while Jesus said I had to go back, and I asked why. He said I had more to do, but I didn't want to go. Finally, I said, 'Okay, Lord, whatever you want,' and I started getting pulled away from him. It was the most painful thing you can imagine. I changed my mind and pleaded, 'I don't want to go back! I don't want to go back!'"

I asked him if there was anything he could remember that Jesus had taught him or revealed. He seemed to search his mind, but then it came to him: "Oh yes, there's one thing. You know how churches are always fighting and arguing about their differences? All the splits and denominations? Jesus hates that!"

I promised Bob that he would have a chance to share his story with the congregation. He remained in the hospital several more days and was released. The stroke had caused problems, but he was sound in mind and retraining himself for public life.

He and his wife returned to church about six weeks later. I asked him if he was ready to tell his story to the congregation, and he said, "What story?" I later sat down with him and recited verbatim his account to me, and he remembered none of it. Two signs of his experience lingered: one was his solid faith in Christ, and the other was an event I observed during Sunday school. As I walked around checking on the various classes one Sunday, I listened at the door to a discussion Bob was involved in—the subject was death. Bob, formerly so strident and argumentative, gently chimed in: "You don't have to worry about death. There's nothing to be afraid of at all."

I walked in and challenged him: "How do you know that, Bob?"

He looked at me as though I had questioned the most obvious fact in the universe. He seemed to be searching for an answer, or the source of his conviction, and then said, "It's in the Bible!"

I smiled and nodded.

—Noel Anderson, Bakersfield, California

A Cry for Help

My husband died in 1995, and left me in a bit of a mess with the bills and paperwork, all of which he had previously handled. A week after his death, I was looking everywhere in the house for our mortgage payment coupons. Frustrated, I began crying and yelling out to my dead husband, "Why did you do this to me?"

I went to bed, and for some reason I woke up in the middle of the night. I could smell my husband. I sat up in bed and then suddenly had a thought come to me: The mortgage coupons were in a folder in the bookcase behind his desk. I walked to his desk and knew exactly where to look. I had never seen the folder before. Even though he never spoke to me, I could sense him there and I could feel him directing me. I felt him touch me ever so softly, and then he was gone. After that I looked at life differently. The experience helped sustain me through my grief.

—Gunilla Pratt, Rancho Sante Fe, California

A Procession of Protectors

One night when I was five years old, my dad took me up to bed. My bedroom was at the end of the hall, facing the stairs. My bed was along the wall that faced the hallway. I remember walking into the room feeling like I just walked into a freezer. I was afraid and asked my dad not to leave me alone because the room was scary.

My dad reassured me that everything was fine and went to get an angel night-light we had in another room. He plugged it into the wall and left despite my pleas for him to stay. I watched him walk down the hall and out of sight as he descended the stairs. Immediately I saw a fireball come up the stairs and head straight for my room. I huddled under the covers in great fear. After a few moments, I peeked out from underneath the covers. The room still felt as cold as ice to me.

Above me swirling around the ceiling was a glowing red "body-builder" with an angry look on this face. He was very muscular and from his waist down he was a jet stream of red light. He kept within the swirl about my head. He covered the ceiling of my room in a fury of red light and was endless energy as he darted around and around. I dared not move a muscle for fear that he would notice me. He did not seem to be interested in me, and I wanted to keep it that way. I wondered if he even knew I was there. I pinched myself very hard several times to wake myself up from this dream or to see if it was real. I wondered how I would sneak out of bed and get downstairs to get my dad. I did not want to yell and get the being's attention or get up and be noticed. I looked down the hall.

Coming up the stairs was a line of angels! They were little girls with flowing hair to their mid backs. Each carried a single candle in both hands and had a long choir dress to the floor. They glowed with a soft white light. The little girls had solemn looks on their faces and in single file marched slowly up the steps in a procession. They entered the door that led to my parents' room (halfway down the hall). Still not wanting to arouse attention, I decided not to move and to watch the angels until I fell asleep.

Years later, my mom asked me if I remembered the night I saw the angels. Like yesterday, I stated! She told me that I shared the angel story with her the next day. I do not remember doing that. She also went on to explain to me that she said nothing to me at the time because I was too young to understand. But now she wanted to tell me that she had been struggling with a deep depression and that night was the low point. She had gone to bed (earlier than me), and as she lay there, demonic faces flashed above her head. She was struggling and kept praying to the Lord. I did not understand all that as a child, but I told her the next morning that the angels were protecting her.

—Marie McWhorter, Queensbury, New York

Encouraging Encounter

In 1963, I was pastoring my first church in Yakima, Washington. My wife, Barbara, and I had just celebrated our wedding anniversary. We felt very blessed. God had given us a daughter and a son, and the church was growing. A few days after our anniversary, Barbara became ill with what appeared to be a severe case of the flu. When it didn't clear up after four days, I called the doctor and he said to bring her in to the hospital. He checked her over and said he was going to admit her. He wanted to call in a specialist because there appeared to be pressure in the cranium. The next day the specialist showed me an X ray and pointed to a dark spot. "I can't be sure," he said, "but I believe that is an inoperable tumor."

Barbara was in the hospital for two months, critical most of the time, and then the Lord called her home.

About a month after her graduation to heaven, I was downtown with our daughter, Pam, who was three at the time. She said to me,

"Daddy, where were you the day Jesus came to our house?" I started to dismiss her question but realized it was not like her to ask something of that nature. So I began to quiz her.

She described the visitor as dressed in white and talking with her mom while Pam played on the floor with her toys. I asked her what her mother did, and she said, "She talked with Jesus and then she cried a little bit."

The moment Pam mentioned her mother crying, I remembered an afternoon about a month before she became ill. I had been out visiting parishioners and stopped by the house to get something. Barbara met me at the door and was wiping her eyes. I asked if she was okay or if something had happened. Her response was "No, I'm fine. I just had such a good visit with the Lord today."

Not once during her two-month illness did she despair or question why she had gotten ill. You will have to draw your own conclusion as to who came to the house that day. Maybe it was an angel or maybe it was the Lord. I just know that someone prepared her in a supernatural way for what would transpire.

–Leonard DeWitt, Ventura, California

More Work to Do

In 1968 I was diagnosed with acoustic neuroma, a benign tumor near the auditory nerve. From my original diagnosis until a ten-hour operation, the tumor had grown from the size of a fifty-cent piece to that of a small lemon.

The prognosis was unsettling to a twenty-two-year-old in his first pastorate: facial paralysis, total loss of hearing, speech difficulties—and possible death during surgery. Thanks to the answered prayers of many across the nation, I survived the surgery—though with the fulfillment of every worst-case prediction except death.

During a routine change of bandages in the intensive care unit, I suddenly experienced cardiac arrest. My first sensation was of a halo of brilliant light. I was at first in its center and subsequently seemed to hover above. I didn't have any sense of a physical bodily presence; it was as if I was above the scene, looking through the brilliance at the activities in the ICU.

I remember being in a state of total relaxation, as if the Spirit of God was present, calming me. I could see the physicians and nurses working on the patient (me) in a hurried fashion, but I wasn't able to see their efforts in detail. Before the incident was over, I heard a voice saying, "I have more for you to do." Within a minute or two, my heartbeat was restored.

Thankfully, the Great Physician had appointed an earthly physician, a heart specialist, to be working on a patient in the bed next to mine at that exact moment.

—Jerry Brecheisen, Fishers, Indiana

Friends Calling Long Distance

My mother, Eleanor, was in a nursing home—Heritage Manor in Flint, Michigan—awaiting her time to go to heaven. Mother was eighty years old and had been failing for a couple of years. My dad, John, wanted to be near to her to help with her care, so he checked himself into the home to be there day and night.

Mom kept telling him there was a long barrel with a light at the bottom, and voices of her departed friends kept calling her name and telling her they were waiting for her. They told her she would like it when she was with them. This was repeated several times before she went to her final destination with Jesus on November 1, 1975.

—Maurice Kilmer, Alpine, California

"I See Gwamma"

I had just finished speaking at a youth camp in Westcliffe, Colorado, and was heading back to Marion, Indiana, where I served on staff at Lakeview Wesleyan Church. I'd spoken at this camp a couple of times before and decided to take the whole family out this time to enjoy the beauty of the Rocky Mountains. Besides, my mother had died three months earlier, and I dreaded being separated from my three favorite people in the world—my wife and two sons. So I took vacation time and we made that twenty-seven-hour trek together in our little Honda Accord, stopping on the way there and back to see friends, family, and a couple of tourist spots.

After the camp ended that Saturday, July 1, we drove all the way back to Topeka, Kansas, where I had been on staff at Fairlawn Heights Wesleyan Church prior to moving to Indiana. We attended Sunday services and were invited by Ed and Sharon Rotz to join their family for lunch and an afternoon at the pool of one of the parishioners.

At the pool that day, our young boys, Davey and Jono, played well with the older kids there. All of the adults had congregated down at the deep end of the pool while the kids splashed in the shallow end. Davey, at three-and-a-half years old, had already become a decent swimmer. Jono, age nineteen months, wore safety arm floats and was being carefully watched it seemed by a couple of the older girls. So we settled in comfortably to chat with friends.

Suddenly someone screamed, "Jono!" I turned to see him, face-down, in the shallow end with no movement and no pronounced ripples of water around him to indicate he'd ended up like that within the past few seconds.

All of the kids had gotten out of the pool and were snacking at the nearby picnic tables. Jono had taken his safety arm floats off for snack time. He had then slipped away from everyone, unnoticed, to follow a ball that had rolled off the edge of the pool and into the water.

Apparently in reaching to retrieve the ball he fell into the water, and no one knew exactly how long he had been there.

When I heard the scream from one of the older kids, I immediately began to swim to rescue my son. Before I could get there, Ben Rotz (about nine at the time) jumped in the water, grabbed Jono around the waist, and yanked him up the steps of the pool and out of the water. As I saw my son being dragged from the water, I was still a few yards away, trying to run through the shallow end to get there as fast as I could. His face was pale blue, and there was no sign of breathing from his limp body. Having been a lifeguard, I had only seen that look once before. My heart sank.

It was not Jono's day to leave us, though. By the time I got to the steps of the pool, I heard the glorious sounds of coughing, spitting up, and gasping for breath. Life began to come back into his face. Unknowingly, young Ben Rotz had saved Jono's life by yanking hard on his midsection as he dragged him out of the water. Needless to say, we were beyond grateful to still have our son with us.

Soon after the incident, we said our good-byes to friends and hit the road for Chicago, where we would be rendezvousing with our staff at Wrigley Field for a Fourth of July Cubs game. On the way, still rejoicing over Jono's miracle, I talked with the boys about how much fun the day was. After some chit-chat and a moment of silence, Jono piped up, "I fall down."

"Yes, you did, buddy," I said. "And you scared Mommy and Daddy."

Jono then said, "And I see Gwamma too, Daddy!"

My first reaction was surprise since, at his age, and given the long distance we lived from my parents, Jono had only seen my mom a few times in his short life. Before Mom's death, they had been living in Southern California, where Mom was the Dean of Nursing at Azusa Pacific University. The boys spoke with them at least once a week on the phone and we would exchange video clips of the boys' activities and grandparent greetings. But something told me that these were not just offhand, childish words from a kid who barely knew his grandma.

I decided to probe gently. "Who did you see, buddy?"

"I see Gwamma," he repeated.

I felt a lump in my throat and my eyes clouded over with tears. I wasn't sure if this was a conversation I even wanted to continue. Then I felt my wife, Brenda, touch my arm from the passenger seat. She gave me a reassuring smile.

I choked out the next question to Jono. "Are you sure you saw Grandma, little buddy?"

"Uh-huh."

"Where did you see Grandma?" I asked.

"When I fall down. And Gwamma was sad too."

At that moment I envisioned my mother's face with her highly expressive, pleading eyes that always emerged when a subject of urgency or pain was discussed. It was the kind of face that would make a nineteen-month-old child see hurt or sadness.

Barely able to compose myself by this time, I asked, "What did Grandma say to you, Jono?"

"She say, 'Swim now, Jono! Swim!'"

I don't know how to explain what my son saw that day. But I often wonder if his vision of his Grandma was what kept him from panicking and filling his lungs with irreversible amounts of water, thus leaving enough earthly life for Ben to yank him up and inadvertently jump-start his drowning little body. Or did he actually catch a glimpse of the other side where his Grandma encouraged him to stay on this earth a while longer?

—David Blackburn, Brevard, North Carolina

Afterword

Jim Garlow

Thank you for allowing us to be your tour guides for the past couple hundred pages. Let us share some final thoughts before this journey ends.

We do hope you will check out the detailed biblical overviews provided in our first book on this topic, *Heaven and the Afterlife*. It has a more detailed exploration of the scriptural underpinnings of our beliefs.

Following is a brief part-by-part review of the basis for this book.

Part 1: Eyewitness Accounts

We believe that God by his grace has given many people glimpses into the spectacular reality of heaven as they "passed over" and "came back." One reason this seems to happen with much greater frequency in our era is because of advances in modern technology, which allow many more people to be resuscitated than in decades and centuries past. These reports affirm what Scripture teaches about the splendors that await those who know the Lord.

But not all afterlife accounts are wonderful and beautiful. Some reveal the horrors of hell. While not as widely reported, they are just as real. Universalists—those that believe *all* will go to heaven—disbelieve these stories. One doctor's extensive research confirms that unless the stories are gathered immediately after the near-death experience, the story is most frequently lost forever, unable to be recalled a few days later.

Scripture states that the way to destruction (hell) is wide and broad while the road to life (heaven) is narrow. These verses should be taken seriously.[1]

Part 2: Someone to Watch Over Me

We believe that angels actually exist, and that some persons have seen them.

Part 3: Mischief-Makers

We believe the Scriptures teach that demons exist and that they do, on occasion, manifest their ugliness. The great news is that those who believe in Jesus have authority over them and therefore need not fear them.

Part 4: Fond Farewells

We recognize that, like Stephen in the New Testament, some are given a unique glimpse of heaven as they are exiting this earth. Those glimpses are in full alignment with what the Bible explicitly teaches regarding the afterlife.

Part 5: Many Happy Returns

As coauthors, we had many discussions about the fifth section in this book, and we readily acknowledge that the topic of "visitations" represents perhaps the most controversial aspect of any afterlife discussion. Indeed, many people struggle with, or even scoff at, the notion that some deceased persons could "cross back over" into this world.

However, if we were going to be honest with the many reports we accumulated, we could not simply ignore this challenging subject. Thus, in the end, we decided to include some of these remarkable, and at times inexplicable, accounts. We do not feel a need to explain what was reported to us. However, it might be advantageous for us to provide some framework for understanding what we ascertained.

As we've stated elsewhere, it is imperative that one never attempt to contact the dead. To do this is not merely to violate the Word of God but to invite deception, at best, and destruction, at worst. Nevertheless, there is apparently no biblically stated prohibition that blocks deceased persons from revisiting this planet they once fully occupied. Like Moses' and Elijah's post-death visit to this earth, there are reliable reports of persons unexpectedly seeing their recently deceased loved ones.

After vetting these types of accounts from credible and rational persons, we have developed a type of grid—unscientific, anecdotal-based observations. What was universally reported was that:

- The living person was surprised by the appearance or visitation of the recently deceased. In other words, they did not seek such a visitation.

- The living person was not frightened by the visit of the recently deceased. In fact, the visit brought comfort regarding the reality of an afterlife and of heaven.

- The visit vastly reduced the fear of death.
- The visit advanced the needed emotional healing among the living, in some cases bringing full and complete healing.
- The visit was typically a one-time event.

In contrast to the characteristics listed above, there are indicators when such a visitation is spiritually untrustworthy and dangerous. A demonic presence masquerading as a deceased relative is referred to as a *familiar spirit*, something to be avoided. Some possible ways to know that the visitation or apparition is demonic is when any one of the following is present:

- The living persons have pursued contact with the dead.
- The living persons were frightened or terrified by the visitation, or described it as eerie. This would be in contrast to the stories presented in previous pages, in which the living persons felt remarkable peace and calmness.
- The living persons came away from the encounter with an anti-biblical belief in Universalism—that is—*all persons* are automatically destined for heaven.
- The living persons attempt to solicit some new truth or information from the deceased. It is at this point that Satan's deceptive powers are manifested. Truth is to be received from God's Word, not from deceased loved ones.

Neither of us began writing our two books on heaven and the afterlife with any thought that we would encounter such stories. In fact, we were originally skeptical of the accounts, until we began seeing the repeated patterns in these reports. Most convincing to us was the fact that their accounts did not violate any Scripture and that these were reported by people in whom we had strong confidence.

The same week that this book was being completed, I (Jim) was being interviewed by a major Christian network. After we went off the air, I hesitatingly ventured to reveal that our newest book contained accounts of these visitations.

I watched the facial reactions of the host and co-host as I explained our discoveries, wondering what their response might be. Before I could finish my explanation, the co-host interrupted me and said, "I know exactly what you are talking about. My father died in 1977. A short time after his death, he appeared to me."

Having heard this type of account numerous times, I responded, "And let me guess—you were not frightened when it happened and you were significantly healed emotionally due to that visit. Right?"

He looked quite surprised, as if I had taken the words right out of his mouth. "Yes. How did you know?"

"Because I have heard this so many times," I responded.

Part 6: Do You Believe in Ghosts?

Leaving this aspect of positive visitations, we do believe that many so-called "ghost" accounts involve demonic activity. The fact that they are eerie or scary—instead of comforting and reassuring—places them in the suspect column.

Part 7: An Eye Toward Eternity

Finally, like the prophets of old, we believe that visions and signs can be a method God uses to communicate with us. He will never communicate something contrary to Scripture. In fact, if a dream or vision or sign is, in any way, counter to the revealed Word of God, it should be regarded as untrustworthy. However, just as God has used visions and signs during biblical times, he can use them today.

As a final thought, we can say that gathering and presenting the stories in this collection—and thinking deeply about many aspects related to the afterlife—has bolstered our faith in and love for our heavenly Father, the Creator of heaven and earth and all things in between. Though we certainly believed in heaven before undertaking this project, we now even more enthusiastically and confidently embrace the reality of a future heaven. To put it mildly, through this experience we grew to more deeply love God and his Word. We hope and pray that this book, along with our previous one on the topic, will have the same influence on you.

Acknowledgments

We owe a debt of gratitude to the hundreds of people who responded to our request for stories of spiritual encounters. Each account represents a significant personal and spiritual event, and we deeply appreciate those men and women for having entrusted their stories to us.

Special thanks to Tracy Burger and Pam Dahl—without whose support I would not be able to do what I do.

And heartfelt gratitude to my wife, children, extended family, and my church family, all of whom patiently support me during the "birth pains" of each new book.

–Jim

This book would not have been possible without the invaluable contributions of my close friend and colleague Alan Wartes, whose enormous creative skills are matched by his integrity and devotion to truth-telling. Strategic help was also provided by Karen Linamen and Jim Lund, who invested their time and talents to see this book through.

Another close friend, Kyle Duncan with Bethany House, championed this project from the beginning and encouraged its development at each phase. Julie Smith patiently put up with pleas for additional writing time and answered endless questions. Our editor, Ellen Chalifoux, provided sound judgment and clear insights to sharpen and hone the manuscript.

Last, but far from least, a thousand thank-yous to my family—Robin, Juliana, and Logan—for enduring my crazy hours and constant stress as I wrote this manuscript. I offer you my unending love and gratitude.

—Keith

Notes

Adventures in the Afterlife

1. Dinesh D'Souza, *Life After Death* (Washington, D.C.: Regnery Publishing Inc., 2009), 3.
2. 1 John 4:16, 18 NKJV
3. Ecclesiastes 11:5
4. John 3:16–17

Doubter . . . or Questioner?

1. In 1976, as a graduate student writing my doctoral dissertation on the eighteenth-century revivalist John Wesley, I was touring England alone for a time before joining up with a group of seventy other Americans. I took the long train ride north from London, followed by a lengthy cab ride with an accompanying expensive fare—at least for a poor student—to the Lincolnshire town of Epworth. There I visited the boyhood home of the famous John Wesley, receiving a delightful privately guided tour of the two-story structure built in 1709 after the Wesley family suffered a frightening house fire.

    The curator, knowing my desire for detail, enthusiastically included a full explanation regarding the house's long-term, active ghost, Old Jeffrey, the name affectionately given it by Samuel Wesley, his wife, Susanna, and their children.

    As the tour ended, it was apparent that darkness was coming soon on that cold October British evening. The curator, knowing I was a long distance from any motel, graciously informed me that persons were allowed to pay a small fee and stay overnight in what would otherwise be an empty house. The fact that it was a rainy night likely only increased my apprehension. Knowing quite well the many Old Jeffrey stories, I quickly declined, fumbling for some excuse as to why I needed to get back to London. Thus I missed my *primo* opportunity for an encounter with one of the world's most documented apparitions!

2. John 20:25
3. Mark 9:24

Part One: Eyewitness Accounts

1. Maurice Rawlings, *To Hell and Back* (Nashville: Thomas Nelson, 1993), 22.
2. Jeffrey Long, *Evidence of the Afterlife: The Science of Near-Death Experiences* (New York: HarperCollins, 2010), 34.
3. John 14:2

Chapter 2: "An Angel Picked Me Up and We Flew"

1. Psalm 18:16, 19
2. Pokémon is the anglicized name for a collection of Japanese anime cartoon characters popular in the United States. It is the contraction of two words, "Pocket Monster." (*Pokémon,* Wikipedia: The Free Encyclopedia, *http://en.wikipedia.org/wiki/Pokemon.*)

Chapter 4: Road Trip to Redemption

1. See Philippians 4:7.
2. Isaiah 6:5

Part Two: Someone to Watch Over Me

1. Some of this is taken from our previous book, *Heaven and the Afterlife* (Minneapolis: Bethany House, 2009). For more detailed information about angels, see chapter 8 of that book.
2. Psalm 148:2–5
3. Psalm 8:5
4. See Daniel 10:5; Matthew 28:3; Revelation 15:6.

5. Revelation 4:6–8
6. F. Forrester Church, quoted in: *Leadership*, vol. 9, no. 3.
7. Hebrews 13:2

Part Three: Mischief-Makers

1. C. S. Lewis, *The Screwtape Letters* (New York: Touchstone, 1942, 1961, 1996), 61.
2. Ibid., 75.
3. Ibid., 47.
4. Ibid., 171.
5. Lewis, ix.
6. Ibid., 6.
7. Some of this material is adapted from *Heaven and the Afterlife*. For a full description of how demons afflict and possess people, see *Heaven and the Afterlife* (Minneapolis: Bethany House, 2009), 116–129.

Chapter 10: Dueling in the Dark

1. Ephesians 6:12

Chapter 11: Evil Comes Home to Roost

1. Matthew 8:28–34

Chapter 13: Kitchen Table Conflict

1. 1 John 4:3–4

Part Four: Fond Farewells

1. Acts 6:15
2. Acts 7:55–58
3. 2 Samuel 12:22–23

Part Five: Many Happy Returns

1. "A Conversation with Frederick Buechner," *Image: A Journal of Arts and Religion* (Spring 1989): 56–57.

2. Deuteronomy 18:10–11

3. Isaiah 8:19–20 NLT

4. For information about this study, see: Dianne Arcangel, *Afterlife Encounters: Ordinary People, Extraordinary Experiences* (Charlottesville, VA: Hampton Roads Publishing Company, 2005).

5. Matthew 17:1–4

6. Hebrews 12:1

Part Six: Do You Believe in Ghosts?

1. Mark Twain, *The Adventures of Tom Sawyer* (New York: Harper & Brothers, 1917), 80.

2. Brian Righi, *Ghosts, Apparitions and Poltergeists: An Exploration of the Supernatural Through History* (Woodbury, MN: Llewellyn Publications, 2008), 88.

3. For a fuller discussion on the subject, see our book *Heaven and the Afterlife*, chapter 5, "Things That Go Bump in the Night: Yes, Virginia, There Really Could Be Ghosts in the Attic."

Part Seven: An Eye Toward Eternity

1. Acts 9:3–8

Chapter 26: "Tonight I'm Going to Take You to Heaven"

1. See Job 13:15.

Afterword

1. Matthew 7:13–14

About the Authors

DR. JIM GARLOW, author, communicator, commentator, and senior pastor of Skyline Church in San Diego, is heard daily on over 800 radio outlets nationwide in his one-minute commentary "The Garlow Perspective." In addition, he airs a 30-minute broadcast called "The Garlow Perspective Special." Garlow is also the chairman of ReAL (Renewing American Leadership), based in Washington, DC.

Due to the success of *Cracking Da Vinci's Code* (coauthored with Peter Jones, nearly 450,000 copies in print, becoming No. 17 on the *New York Times* Bestsellers List–paperback, nonfiction), Jim has appeared regularly on NBC, CNN, Fox, MSNBC, and CNBC. This book, *Encountering Heaven and the Afterlife,* is a response to the success of Dr. Garlow's 2009 book with Keith Wall entitled *Heaven and the Afterlife.* Other books by Jim Garlow include *How God Saved Civilization* (re-released as *God and His People*), *A Christian's Response to Islam, The Covenant, Partners in Ministry, The 21 Irrefutable Laws of Leadership Tested by Time,* and *God Still Heals.* Jim's books have been translated into ten languages.

Jim's wife, Carol, serves as Minister of Prayer and Intercession at Skyline Wesleyan Church. Jim and Carol have four children and five grandsons.

For more information, please visit *www.jimgarlow.com.*

KEITH WALL, a twenty-year publishing veteran, writes full time in collaboration with several bestselling authors. He lives with his family in Colorado Springs.

You've read the stories— but what should you believe?

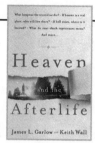